CW00919631

PRACTICAL WISDOM

PRACTICAL WISDOM

Thinking Differently About
College and University Governance

Peter D. Eckel and Cathy A. Trower

Foreword by Richard Chait

Copublished with

STERLING, VIRGINIA

COPYRIGHT © 2019 BY STYLUS PUBLISHING, LLC.

Published by Stylus Publishing, LLC.
22883 Quicksilver Drive
Sterling, Virginia 20166-2019

All rights reserved. No part of this book may be reprinted or reproduced in any form or by any electronic, mechanical or other means, now known or hereafter invented, including photocopying, recording, and information storage and retrieval, without permission in writing from the publisher.

Library of Congress Cataloging-in-Publication Data
Names: Eckel, Peter D., author. | Trower, Cathy A. (Cathy Ann), author.
Title: Practical wisdom : thinking differently about college and university governance / Peter D. Eckel and Cathy A. Trower; foreword by Richard Chait.
Description: First edition. | Sterling, Virginia : Stylus Publishing, LLC., 2018.
Includes bibliographical references and index.
Identifiers: LCCN 2018016890 (print) | LCCN 2018034147 (ebook) | ISBN 9781620368404 (Library networkable e-edition) | ISBN 9781620368411 (Consumer e-edition) | ISBN 9781620368398 (paperback : acid free paper) | ISBN 9781620368381 (cloth : acid free paper)
Subjects: LCSH: Universities and colleges--United States--Administration. | College administrators--United States. | College trustees--United States.
Classification: LCC LB2341 (ebook) | LCC LB2341 .E265 2018 (print) | DDC 378.1/011--dc23
LC record available at https://lccn.loc.gov/2018016890

13-digit ISBN: 978-1-62036-838-1 (cloth)
13-digit ISBN: 978-1-62036-839-8 (paperback)
13-digit ISBN: 978-1-62036-840-4 (library networkable e-edition)
13-digit ISBN: 978-1-62036-841-1 (consumer e-edition)

Printed in the United States of America

All first editions printed on acid-free paper
that meets the American National Standards Institute
Z39-48 Standard.

Bulk Purchases
Quantity discounts are available for use in workshops and for staff development.
Call 1-800-232-0223

First Edition, 2019

To Corinne Eckel,
who represents the future generation of
students, for whom trustees govern
Peter D. Eckel

To Steven Charles Eggert,
my amazing brother, who has taught
me more than he'll ever realize
Cathy A. Trower

CONTENTS

TABLES AND FIGURES

Tables

Figures

FOREWORD

S he was always professionally attired. She had a competitive edge, a disciplined approach, and an MBA in hand. He donned the garb of a graduate student. He had ample empathy, a lively mind that caromed from one concept to another, and a master's degree in counseling and personnel services. Despite their differences, they clicked as classmates. They liked to joust, ever appreciative that their encounters made them both smarter. I was the professor. They were the "go-to" students to provoke and advance discussions of the case studies we dissected.

That was 1994 in the higher education doctoral program at the University of Maryland, College Park. At the time, Cathy A. Trower and Peter D. Eckel were notably talented students with enormous potential. Today they are reigning experts on college and university governance, and I am a proud mentor.

This book, a powerful admixture of compatibly divergent thinkers, combines the intellectual horsepower of researchers with the street smarts they gathered over nearly a quarter century as practitioners and consultants. The result is indeed *Practical Wisdom*, an insightful and instructive suite of chapters that makes you think and helps you govern at a time when governance truly matters.

In the mid-1970s, when I started to examine trusteeship, that was not the case. In fact, when asked what I studied, I had to enunciate "*gov-er-NANCE.*" Otherwise I was likely to be identified as a professor of *gov-ern-MENT.* Today college and university governance occupies center stage, positioned there by a litany of problems: an unsustainable business model, public dissatisfaction with costs and results, student consumerism and activism, and demands for greater accountability. And that's before boards tackle the complexities of shared governance, academic medicine, funded research, intercollegiate athletics, global competition, and student life.

In short, trusteeship matters as never before. The stakes are high and the challenges are manifold. Business as usual will not suffice. To grapple with all these threats (and some opportunities) boards need to do better work and work better. But how does a board do this?

The 16½ chapters that follow offer a superb reference. Taken together the chapters comprise a user's manual for college and university board members. No owner reads a user's manual cover to cover whether for an automobile or an appliance. Rather, we read what's germane when we want to gain more from the product or when a problem arises. That's sensible.

However, given widespread underperformance among college and university boards and the spate of problems trustees confront, this user's manual should not be relegated to the glove compartment or a kitchen drawer. Instead, keep the book nearby and consult the pertinent chapters in order to enrich the board's purposes and effectiveness and avert dysfunction.

There are three levers to enhance a board's performance: (a) content, (b) structure, and (c) culture. Eckel and Trower address all three with a blend of sophisticated concepts and uncomplicated practices. Each chapter exposes and explains the "software" of governance—for example, power, cognition, social dynamics, and organizational culture—and then proposes concrete "applications" to bolster, for example, agenda development, strategy, committees, chair–CEO relations, and performance accountability. Each chapter concludes with a line of inquiry for trustees to pursue that invites reflective practice and continuous improvement.

Many well-intentioned board members start to read a pamphlet or treatise on college governance only to be deterred by abstract theories, impractical recommendations, pretentious prose, or some combination thereof. As one trustee quipped about a tome on trusteeship, "Once you put it down, you can't pick it up." Not so in this case. There's an abundance of relevance peppered with dashes of irreverence—just the right mix for readers to be enlightened, engaged, and bemused. The payoffs for trustees are substantial: more influential deliberations, more consequential contributions, greater fulfillment, and added efficiency.

Boards should leave legacies—not just better governance but stronger institutions. In concert with the administration and faculty, trustees shape institutional aims and ambitions. Governance consultants have no comparative advantage or appropriate role here. *Practical Wisdom* astutely focuses on the means—tools, techniques, and templates—that enable trustees and, by extension, executives to determine, pursue, and achieve a core strategy aligned with core values. There's no more valuable contribution a book on governance can make.

Professors should leave legacies, too, none more important than cultivation of the next generation of scholars. Trower and Eckel were not diamonds in the rough polished by a professor. Both evidenced so much ability as graduate students that their success was inevitable. I claim no credit other than kindling their interest in governance. Fortunately for higher education, both took the bait.

Richard Chait
Professor Emeritus of Higher Education,
Harvard Graduate School of Education

ACKNOWLEDGMENTS

We want to acknowledge the contributions of trustees who volunteer their time, talents, and treasure for the institutions they serve. Higher education in this country and elsewhere is stronger because of the caliber of these individuals. We specifically want to thank the board members and presidents of the various universities and colleges who have invited us into their boardrooms. We deeply appreciate these opportunities to serve as your partners in leadership to improve governance.

We appreciate the contributions of Matt Hartley at the University of Pennsylvania's Graduate School of Education for his thought leadership and contributions to many ideas in this book, particularly related to board culture. We also want to acknowledge the intellectual contributions of our friend, mentor, and former professor, Richard Chait. Throughout our professional lives, he has continued to ask us questions that push us to think deeply and in new ways about higher education and governance. We also are proud and thankful that he penned the foreword to this book on our behalf.

We thank *Inside Higher Ed* for their partnership on this effort. Some of the chapters here first appeared as essays in this important higher education publication. Sarah Bray at *Inside Higher Ed* has been particularly encouraging in the exploration of these ideas and helped us shape their form and focus. We also want to thank our editor, David Brightman at Stylus Publishing, LLC, for his support and advice.

Finally, we thank our families for putting up with our obsession with governance while writing this book, but also before and likely after it. It's a good thing they love us.

INTRODUCTION
Thinking, Doing, Governing

This is a book about helping those involved with governance—board members and administrators—approach their work in new ways. The primary aim of the book is to provide insight that boards can use to enhance their governing practices. We take governance seriously. Given the tone of this book, in places, one might not think that is the case. (We figure a little levity never hurts.) Although there are a good number of other resources for boards, our approach involves thinking differently about governance. Our basic premise is that too many boards are not reaching their full potential because they routinely adopt or continue to use ineffective practices that go unexamined. It's the "just-how-we-do-things-around-here" syndrome. Our contention is that if boards are more intentional in thinking about *what* they do, *how* they do it, and *why* they do it, they will reconsider habitual practices, change some things, reflect on the changes, learn, and govern better—more intentionally. And these efforts will help trustees add more value to the colleges, universities, and state systems they govern. This book is predominantly directed toward higher education, but we think many of its ideas are relevant to governance in other sectors, particularly independent schools, nonprofit organizations, hospitals, and healthcare systems. Some may find it applicable to corporate boards, but this is the sector with which we have the least experience.

We use thought-provoking chapter titles and a conversational tone to engage readers, get them to reflect on their work, and broaden their horizons. Our goal is engaging trustees on issues they find relevant and in ways they find practical and stimulating. We think that boards can and should play a positive, meaningful role in the trajectory of organizations they serve. Effective boards add value and, unfortunately, the reverse is true as well; ineffective boards do not.

We wrote this book based on our experiences in boardrooms; it reflects our lessons learned by serving as trustees, consulting with boards, and studying them through our past and ongoing research efforts. We spend a lot of time working across a set of very different boards at different types of institutions. We see the questions boards are asking, or should be asking, and the thinking that could increase their impact. Having broad views beyond a single boardroom is uncommon; it has helped us see patterns—across boards and over time—about issues that boards should be considering and the cultures in which they are situated. Most trustees, in our experience, serve on a single university board. There are some who serve on multiple boards concurrently or over time, yet most trustees find themselves as novices in complex and often seemingly foreign environments. Issues such as tuition setting (why do our "customers" pay less than it costs to produce our "product?"), tenure and academic freedom (as well as academic prerogative), or strategic planning in a culture of shared governance, to name a few common artifacts of higher education, do not have easy parallels in other sectors or industries. This means that board members may find their attention focused almost exclusively on the work facing the college or university and have little time left to consider how they are to go about governing. We, however, have been thinking about how boards go about their business.

We want boards to not simply go through the paces of governance but instead create an intentional mind-set for how they govern. Given the composition and structure of boards, governance may almost be an unnatural act. First, individuals who serve on boards tend to be highly accomplished in their own diverse roles. Many trustees have served in C-suite positions in other organizations, where they are in charge; translate that mind-set and skill set to the boardroom and you may have "an orchestra of soloists" (Chait, 2006, p. 2). Second, trustees come from a variety of sectors and have different backgrounds; they may be unfamiliar with how others think, act, and solve problems in higher education settings. Third, boards meet infrequently—some only two or three times a year—so governance is episodic, and trustees may be unaware of, or out of step with, events on campus. Fourth, board composition changes; therefore, trustees periodically govern with different people whom they may not know very well, making it difficult to develop into a high-performing team. Finally, boards face full agendas with limited time to devote to complex issues. To overcome these challenges, the best boards are intentional about how they govern because they think about their work.

We frame this book around wisdom for boards. As the old saw goes, trusteeship is about three W's—work, wealth, and wisdom. Both of us volunteer our time as trustees (work) and contribute our wealth as we can. This book focuses on that third W of trusteeship—wisdom. According to *Merriam-Webster's Collegiate Dictionary* (1999), the term *wisdom* has multiple definitions; two are especially germane: (a) "accumulated philosophical or scientific learning"; (b) "a wise attitude or course of action" (p. 1358). Our goal is to synthesize our accumulated learning so that boards can adopt wise courses of action and attitudes toward their work.

Although this is a book about governance, we view governance as the means to a greater end. The goal of good governance is to advance colleges and universities, to make them increasingly and steadfastly relevant social organizations that maximize their missions and have lasting positive impact on their students and communities, and to do this in ways that are financially sustainable over the long run. Higher education is in no way a monolithic sector and governance reflects that. Higher education is diverse, consisting of two- and four-year colleges and universities, both private and public, in the United States and abroad, having broad arrays of degree offerings and missions or narrower aims. As the sector varies, so do boards. Some are very large, encompassing state systems; others are small. Some meet frequently; others infrequently. Our approach presents ideas that, we hope, will speak to a variety of board members at a wide range of colleges, universities, and state systems.

About This Book

We structure this book so that you don't have to read it all, cover to cover, or its chapters in order. Some chapters will be more relevant to some administrators and boards than others. We invite you to skip around from chapter to chapter in any order that best suits your interests and the priorities and governance challenges you face. Governance doesn't have a set order, so why should this book? Boxes like Box I.1 are also intended to be helpful touchstones throughout. The first paragraph of each chapter provides an overview of what is to follow, serving as a prechapter summary.

The primary audiences for this book are the trustees of U.S. universities, colleges, and state systems and the presidents and other administrators who work with these boards. Faculty and students interested in governance may also find this book helpful.

However, we think the book will also have transferability to nonprofit boards beyond higher education. Boards and presidents at universities outside the United States might also find this book relevant—especially those

BOX I.1.
Helpful Hints

We use a few boxes like this to call attention to certain points and helpful vignettes.

in countries undergoing governance reform (e.g., those moving beyond centrally coordinated higher education systems toward more market-based, democratic, or autonomous approaches; greetings to Kazakhstan, Malaysia, India, the United Kingdom, Canada, and Australia—each paying increased or renewed attention to board governance).

In the chapters that follow, we explore a variety of issues boards face and offer our wisdom based on a combined four decades of experience working with public and private college and university leaders and in university board-rooms. You will notice numerous unattributed quotes from trustees and academic leaders that we gleaned from conversations, e-mails, interviews, and board self-assessment survey responses. To protect anonymity, quotes are not attributed to specific individuals; after all, those quoted were not informed that their utterances or written comments would end up in a book. But we are grateful for their insight.

Chapter 1 "The Evolving Board: Ways to Think About Governing Today"

Good governance requires effectiveness across three elements: structure, content (i.e., meeting agendas), and culture. Furthermore, most board work is of three types, considering three points in time: oversight (retrospective), problem-solving (present), and problem-finding (future). Many boards have strong thinking in one or two of these dimensions, but the best boards develop the appropriate balance across all three and reflect that balance in their structure, content, and culture. To help boards think broadly and more succinctly about the types of work they do, this chapter presents our views on the work of boards and offers an alternative way to organize that work.

Chapter 2 "The 'Damned If You Do, Damned If You Don't' Dynamics of Governing"

Some would argue that the deck is stacked against boards working effectively and efficiently. College and university boards are composed of volunteers (many of whom "pay" for the privilege of holding those posts because of expected or required donations) who meet periodically (typically three or four times per year for private university boards). Most trustees do not have experience in higher education. Being a trustee is a difficult volunteer role, and boards often find themselves in "damned if you do, damned if you don't" situations. We use this chapter to highlight a few harsh realities that can make good governance challenging.

Chapter 3 "Is Your Board Mediocre?"

Harvard Business School professor Dutch Leonard (2013) once said, "The central challenge for nonprofit leadership is that mediocrity is survivable." Sad, but true. And this is too often the case for college and university boards. However, given the challenges facing higher education today, mediocrity might not be survivable. The higher education and popular press are replete with stories of not only underwhelming board performance (e.g., South Carolina State, Sweet Briar, The University of Texas at Austin), but also of governance going terribly awry (e.g., Penn State, the University of Virginia). The problem for most boards isn't that they are terrible, but that they are only minimally sufficient. A certain realization has surfaced about too many college and university boards—they are mediocre. This chapter discusses what lies behind mediocrity and how boards can move beyond it.

Chapter 4 "Individual Competencies for Collective Impact"

Much conversation about effective governance is about what boards do as a group, and that's fine; but, as collectives of individuals, the best boards are those where the sum adds up to more than the individual parts. We don't, however, choose a *group* of people for board service; we choose *individuals*. What are, and should be, the competencies of those individuals? In this chapter, we discuss the individual competencies of board members that will help improve how the collective governs.

Chapter 5 "Right Answers; Wrong Questions"

Trustees and presidents expect a lot from governance, yet many know that their boards are underperforming—that the board could and should do more. Asking thoughtful, informed questions is important to that continued improvement. Many calls we've received from presidents and board leaders in the United States and abroad seeking to improve governance include a standard set of questions. Although we applaud the interest, the most commonly asked questions may be the *wrong* ones—for instance, "What is the right number of board members?" "How often should the board meet?" "Do we have the right committees and the right number of committees?" These questions, although somewhat off-target, are well intended. After addressing those questions (and what lies beneath them), we propose (and answer) an alternative set of questions we think boards should discuss.

Chapter 6 "Spending Scarce Time Wisely"

It's no surprise that what happens in board meetings is essential to the impact boards have on the institutions they serve. Time is one of the most precious commodities trustees have and one that, if squandered, can result in trustee disengagement and mediocrity. Ideally, board meetings are events that trustees look forward to as opportunities to add critical insight on the most important issues facing the institution; the president and staff, in turn, look forward to meetings to enrich their thinking. These notions place a premium on the meeting agenda as a tool to ensure efficiency and effectiveness. This chapter offers ideas to help institutions get the most from meetings by being intentional about outcomes and structuring activities to achieve stated goals.

Chapter 7 "Ensuring Accountability for the Board by the Board"

The headlines show that no type of institution is exempt from governance woes and sometimes the intervention of attorneys general, governors, alumni, and others when things get particularly troublesome. At the heart of many of these situations is the challenge of board accountability. What is accountability when it comes to governance? To whom are boards accountable and for what? And how can they improve their accountability? The student learning movement has increased the emphasis on faculty accountability. Accreditation addresses institutional accountability. Board accountability has yet to garner the same attention. This chapter highlights how boards can get ahead of the accountability curve and, by so doing, greatly help their institutions.

Chapter 8 "Curiosity: The Boardroom's Missing Element"

Good boards ask good questions; great boards ask great questions. The ability to ask meaningful questions is an important skill in the boardroom and fundamental to effective governance—as noted in the following quote from the chapter by a corporate chairman: "The most distinguished board is useless and does a real disservice to the organization, in my view, if the people on it don't ask the right questions. If you're not asking questions, you're not doing your job" (Dowling, 2009). Too many boards struggle with asking questions at all, let alone asking good or great ones. Statements, not questions, frequently carry the day. Why? This chapter argues that some boards lack sufficient curiosity, but by asking effective questions, they can develop that competency.

Chapter 9 "The 'Jobs' of Committees: Of Drill Bits and Milkshakes"

Committees are where many boards get most of their work accomplished. But committees can do more and have greater impact. Unfortunately, too many boards are not sufficiently intentional about the work of committees and how one committee might work differently than another within the same board. The chapter notes Harvard Business School professor Theodore Levitt, who says that people don't buy a drill bit because they want a drill bit; they buy it because they want a hole. Levitt and other organizational scholars argue that one should look for the "jobs" people seek to accomplish rather than just their behaviors. Board committees perform certain "jobs," and different committees present a mix of jobs. Knowing the mix of what jobs different types of committees can and should do can help boards better use their committees, stay out of the weeds, and increase their focus on what matters most in terms of oversight and strategic imperatives.

Chapter 10 "The Culture of Boards: Making the Invisible Visible"

Governing boards are dynamic groups of individuals where, sometimes, the whole does not equal the sum of the parts. Presidents want and need their boards to be active, productive, and engaged assets for the university, college, or state system they govern, yet too many boards underperform. Educating boards on *what* they should do—their roles and responsibilities—although important, is insufficient. Underperforming boards may know their roles but have cultures that limit their effectiveness. Board culture, those patterns of behavior and ways of understanding that are deeply engrained, reinforced, and taught to new trustees, is what demands attention. It has been said that culture eats structure and strategy for lunch, and we agree. But board culture is much more elusive and difficult to explain succinctly, making it a challenge to expose and to leverage constructively. This chapter focuses on making invisible board culture visible and actionable.

Chapter 11 "The (Not So) Hidden Dynamics of Power and Influence"

Because boards are groups of people, social dynamics come into play. An important dynamic is the balance, or imbalance, of power within the board. Boardroom power comes from a variety of sources, including the obvious—experience, knowledge, and expertise—and less obvious—participation, information, and the ability to control rewards and coercion (think philanthropy). Understanding the sources and balance of power is the window into explaining much about how boards behave, and with a greater understanding, they can improve the outcomes they seek to achieve.

Chapter 12 "The Prime Partnership Between Presidents and Board Chairs"

The president and board chair have a complex relationship. It includes oversight, in which the board is the president's boss and supervisor; strategic partnership, in which the board and by extension the chair collaborate with the president and serve as thought partner(s); and the role of colleague, considering that the presidency is a lonely post and chairs can be the friendly port in the storm. The difficulty is that all three roles are simultaneously in play, and some chairs are better at some of these roles than others. This chapter explores those dynamics and offers insight on how to create a constructive relationship. To make matters more complicated, the relationships, as drivers, are fluid. Some changes are expected, but some are less so, requiring chairs and presidents to change the way they work and engage across the three modes described.

Chapter 13 "Creating the Capacity for Trying Issues"

Boards face a series of challenges over time; they have the capacity and wherewithal to deal with some, but not necessarily all. Trying issues require boards to develop new capacities, enact new structures, and alter the focus of their work. Issues of diversity and inclusivity (and often student activism) are timely and relevant examples of trying issues. Although boards have a significant leadership role to play, they are rarely poised to engage appropriately the challenging issues that most vex institutional leaders. Addressing the issues of diversity, equity, and inclusion is difficult for a host of reasons specific to these types of issues, including (a) the composition (mostly White males) of boards, (b) difficulties framing the issues for action, and (c) the complexity of the issue itself. Difficulties are also due to such common governance shortcomings as (a) lack of sophistication on student and faculty issues in general; (b) insufficient use of data, metrics, and dashboards; and (c) the pull of competing issues. In this chapter, we explore ways to improve a board's capacity to deal with big challenges.

Chapter 14 "Strategy, Higher Education, and Boards (and Forget Planning)"

All institutions have strategic plans, yet few have boards that agree that the plan is meaningful and consequential—that it has real impact on what happens or that it is an effective road map for the future, especially during turbulent times of rapid change. Strategic plans should be about intentional, institutional change. In the end, some plans become guiding documents that provide direction on paths forward, but many do not. In the minds of many trustees, the return on investment of all the effort put into strategic planning is seriously low. Although many boards encourage new approaches to planning, improving *planning* might very well be the wrong focus. In this chapter we argue that institutions and boards should focus on *strategy*, not *planning*.

Chapter 15 "Getting to Grips With Shared Governance"

Trustees new to serving on the boards of colleges and universities some-times feel as though they've entered an alien world, with Byzantine structures, outdated business models, and strange practices like lifetime employment for tenured faculty. And long-serving trustees wonder why they are still surprised and confused by all of this. Among the oddest features of academia is shared governance. Why would those with legal authority, and who are ultimately accountable for the enterprise, delegate responsibility in diffuse fashion to employees? This chapter addresses that question.

Chapter 16 "Governing Circa 1749"

As college and university boards seek strategies for more effective governance, they look to many places—other university boards, hospitals and nonprofit organizations, and corporate boards. However, looking backward to history can also prove fruitful to find solutions to today's, and even tomorrow's, chal-lenges. The University of Pennsylvania's board started meeting in 1749 and kept a set of minutes. Those handwritten minutes reveal much more than Benjamin Franklin's signature; they provide lessons that even 269 years later are instructive to today's trustees. They offer common sense on university governance even before Thomas Paine wrote (a very different) *Common Sense* about a different type of governance.

Chapter 16½ "Half a Chapter: The Unfinished Work"

Boards are sometimes admonished to get governance right. Although that might seem a noble goal, it isn't quite on the mark. As the chapters in this volume demonstrate, governance is a constant work in progress. Rarely is there a "right" for boards to get. Instead, boards must keep working toward improvement and being intentional about their work. So why label the conclusion only half a chapter? We do this because the ideas in this book tell only part of the story. The rest remains to be written by each board as it moves into the future. The completion of the chapter, the final one in this book, is the ongoing work of the board, its leaders, and the administration with which it partners. We invite you to draft the remainder of this chapter through the work you do, the questions about governance you pose, and the intentionality and tenacity that you demonstrate.

Conclusion

We are confident that boards will find ways to apply the practical ideas presented in this comprehensive set of focused chapters. Boards are essential to institutional well-being, and the work is challenging enough and complex enough not to be taken for granted. Wisdom matters in the boardroom. Boards can be important thought partners for presidents and other senior administrators, while serving as conduits to worlds beyond higher education, adding prestige, helping broker important connections, and bringing a depth and perspective to the strategic discussions of the direction of the college, university, state system, or nonprofit organization. Many also contribute wealth. Boards are well positioned to get above the fray of day-to-day institutional operations and focus on long-term institutional viability. To govern well takes work, intentionality, and sustained commitment.

THE EVOLVING BOARD

Ways to Think About Governing Today

Good governance requires effectiveness across three elements: structure, content (i.e., meeting agendas), and culture. Furthermore, most board work is of three types, considering three points in time: oversight (retrospective), problem-solving (present), and problem-finding (future). Many boards are strong in one or two of these dimensions, but the best boards develop an appropriate balance across all three and reflect that balance in their structure, content, and culture. To help boards think broadly and more succinctly about the types of work they do, this chapter presents our views on the work of boards and offers an alternative way to organize that work.

Three Scenarios of Boards in Transition

The work of boards can be complex and often challenging. Real boards face real problems as highlighted in the following three scenarios.

Scenario One

The 24-member board of a residential liberal arts college has worked in crisis mode for the past 3 years. The board had to remove a president after enrollments and financial health took abrupt turns for the worse following several years of slow decline. (Said one trustee, "The ship never turned." Another chimed in more cynically, "Instead, it just sank faster.") The first interim president was a poor fit and left shortly after he started. The faculty were upset about the lack of transparency with the previous administrations over the financial situation and the selection of the interim. The interim president never had the full support of the campus or the board; he was mostly a convenient "placeholder" hire. The faculty placed a good deal of blame for the

failed interim president on the board. The institution seemed to be progressing in the wrong direction.

Simultaneously, the board was wrestling with leadership transitions of its
own, the institution's financial and enrollment problems, and an increasingly
discontented faculty. Now with more stable presidential leadership, the institution is turning a corner. It has embarked on new enrollment strategies that
are, so far, surpassing expectations. The board has created bridges to not only
faculty leadership but with all the college's 125 faculty. ("We've been to *a lot*
of meetings," said the board chair.) Having made it through this unsettling
period, the board no longer needs to operate in crisis mode. The question
board leadership is asking is "How do we approach our work differently now
that the crisis is behind us?"

Scenario Two

An urban university that offers a mix of undergraduate and professional master's programs recruited a new president—an experienced fund-raiser from
another local, more prestigious university. The new president is succeeding an individual who served as president for 23 years and who spent his
entire career at the university, ascending from the rank of assistant professor.
He was ill during the last 2 years of his presidency and eventually resigned
at the personal insistence of the former board chair. The board, consisting of 32 trustees, has a board meeting attendance and trustee engagement
problem. At best, three-quarters of trustees attend any given board meeting.
Board meetings are short—typically a few hours—and happen 4 times a
year. Participation on committees is also underwhelming. Committees meet
episodically, convened at the discretion of the committee chair. Under the
past administration, committees met when prompted by the president with
specific issues he wanted addressed. The new president and the long-term
board chair recognize that the board is not adding much value. Most trustees
seem to agree; although their views are unstated, the attendance record (and
philanthropic contributions) is evidence. The question the new president
and board chair have is "How do we approach our work differently now after
a decade of board complacency?"

Scenario Three

A regional public university was in growth mode, greatly expanding its physical plant through new real estate acquisitions in an economically depressed
part of the state. The master plan includes renovating existing buildings
into residence halls and constructing new classrooms, but it seems that the
nine-member board was overly engaged in this work. Said the executive vice

president, "The trustees need to understand their role, what it means to be a public board in an autonomous state." Confusion about management versus governance began during the development of the campus master plan under the previous president. Before the master planning effort, the board was underengaged ("mostly by design of the prior president," said the current president). As many of the trustees had real estate development experience, and master planning and construction are in their sweet spots, the then-president saw the master plan as a way to generate more trustee engagement with the university. However, during this time, the institution ran into financial challenges. The board thought it needed to step up its oversight responsibility, which it did, not only in terms of finances and the master plan, but across all of its work. The current president wonders, "How do we get the board to rethink its role—away from managing and back to governing?"

These three cases are different, yet they share a common need: to evolve the work of the board to fit today's challenges, not yesterday's. Each of these boards had developed habits and patterns of work over time that had gone unexamined until now. Each was responding to pressing institutional challenges and opportunities over a period of time. The needs now have changed, and the governing boards must evolve their work. Boards that add value know that although some governance work is regular—anticipated and steadfast—other work is not. Context changes, new needs emerge, crises grab attention, complacency sets in—and a board's work should evolve. The question is "How do boards progress in ways that keep pace with, if not get out ahead of (but not too far), the institutions they govern?"

Board Effectiveness: Structure, Content, Culture

As the three examples illustrate, good governance is context- and work-specific. What once worked for a board may no longer suffice. As boards work to keep pace with what's needed of them today and into the future, it is helpful to consider three elements of effective governance—structure, content, and culture (see Figure 1.1).

Structure

Structure, the first and most common point of focus, encompasses board size; committees and task forces; meeting frequency; term limits and trustee evaluation; orientation and onboarding new trustees; means of communications (e.g., electronic board books/portals); and leadership (officers and committee chairs) succession processes. Boards should periodically revisit these

Figure 1.1. Three elements of effective boards.

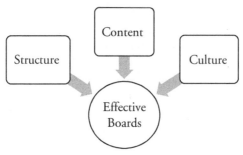

elements by asking, "Do our current structures work for us?" But a warning: Although structure is important, structural changes alone typically will not remedy governance shortcomings. See chapter 5 on questions boards should be asking and chapter 10 on culture for more discussion on this point.

Atop the list of structural questions most asked by boards is "How many trustees should we have?" Boards vary tremendously in size. On average, private university boards have 29 trustees and public boards have 12 (Association of Governing Boards [AGB], 2016). We have worked with boards ranging from as small as 5 trustees to as large as 75 (and some boards are even larger). The fact is "most small boards want to be larger and most large boards want to be smaller" (Chait, 2009, p. 10). Although there may be good reasons to grow the board larger (typically philanthropy, but also breadth of knowledge), there are challenges associated with big boards. Generally, as boards get larger, trustee engagement wanes and presidents may lose an important strategic thought partner. The question is not "Should we be smaller or larger," but instead, "*Why* should we change our size?" Logical next questions are "How large/small should we be to accomplish what?" and "How do we best move in that direction?"

Wisdom from the corporate sector is that boards should be comparatively small. The *Wall Street Journal* (about corporate boards) suggested that smaller (seven to nine) is better when it comes to total shareholder return (Lublin, 2014), but this may not be true in higher education where there are *stake*holders rather than *share*holders. Some colleges, universities, and state systems may benefit from large boards (see Box 1.1) which provide more hands to do the work (e.g., fill committees) and more heads to offer broader and more diverse perspectives on issues and provide a larger network to advance institutional objectives (including, of course, a bigger fund-raising pool of deeply engaged and knowledge people). However, small boards may be able to reach consensus more easily, they may be more responsive, and they may

BOX 1.1.
Unexpected Benefit of a Large Board

At a particular university, when the campus administration was surprised by a well-organized off-campus collective bargaining effort of its adjunct faculty, the president with a 32-person board was able to quickly call on trustees from diverse industries with unions for advice and counsel. Board members had not been selected for this particular experience, but their quick and insightful input proved very helpful. In this instance, a large board had capacity and knowledge that served the institution well in an unexpected situation.

be able to involve their members in more meaningful work. Yet more weight falls upon the shoulders of fewer trustees.

Overall, board size may not matter in and of itself; it is dependent upon how the board uses its committees and its time. Some boards are "board-centric," where most of the work is done by the full board. Other boards are "committee-centric," where most of the heavy lifting happens in committees. What seems to matter most is having expectations align with size. We've seen larger boards have very strong committees. And we've seen small boards rely less on their committees and more on the board as a whole. The problems arise when these 2 approaches do not align. Larger boards that are board-based risk inefficiency, among other challenges, and small boards that are committee-based risk coordination problems (too few people are spread across a set of committees) as well as overloading individuals with too much work. One modest-sized board (with 24 trustees) we know of assigned each trustee to 3 different committees. When they added the meetings of 3 committees to the 4 full-board meetings each year, trustees found they were quite taxed for time (and the president's staff was inordinately busy planning for, attending, and cleaning up after meetings).

An important question regarding board size is "Why change?" Too often board size is a classic solution in search of a problem (Cohen & March, 1986), or it might be the wrong solution for a poorly diagnosed problem. Understanding the gains (and the *governance* gains, not simply the *philanthropic* ones) is a starting point for boards wanting to grow. For boards wanting to shrink, exploring what fewer fully engaged trustees might mean is important (and it's not simply to remove the deadwood from the board as there are other ways to do that—term limits, rigorous evaluations, etc.).

Finally, how to change. Boards are composed of individuals with expectations, commitments, and egos. Facilitating a board reduction can risk alienating deep supporters of the institution if not done intentionally and carefully.

Growth can risk a "Wild West" approach to recruitment. We've all heard of boards that grow in preparation for a comprehensive campaign, which may leave boards with new members seeking the gains and goals of philanthropy without understanding or prizing their fiduciary roles. (See Chait [2009] for a discussion of "the allure of philanthropy over governance" [p. 4].) Those boards need a thorough vetting and orientation process for the cohort of new trustees to set expectations around their fiduciary role. Understanding why boards are making the change is important but so is the process of change.

Content

The second component of board effectiveness that must work in concert with structure is content—what boards spend their time on. This is the substance of the work. Many boards focus on the wrong issues or allocate the wrong amount of time to the right issues. Trower (2013) provides a set of questions for boards to consider related to the substance of meeting agendas, including the following: "What do we want to achieve at this meeting? How do we best structure the meeting to get those results? Where can board members add value?" (p. 144).

Designing effective board meeting agendas requires identifying the salient topics, given the timing of the meeting, and allocating enough time for their exploration. Not all board discussions need to end in a decision. There are many other noble aims, including but not limited to educating the board on complex issues, allowing the president to "think aloud" or float a trial balloon with the board, taking the board's pulse on an important matter, and asking trustees to think broadly about trends affecting the campus. Chapter 6 is about effective meetings. (A hint of what's to come: Too many boards take agenda development too lightly.)

Culture

The third and final component of our baseline for effective boards is culture. Of the three areas, this is the most challenging to understand and act upon (and thus we spend an entire chapter on this topic—chapter 10). Simply stated, *culture* is the "way things are done around here." Although the concept of culture can seem elusive, and not all agree about what it is (despite all agreeing that it matters), its various definitions tend to include aspects such as shared understandings and interpretations of events that guide behavior, or the implicit and explicit rules that shape social interaction (Martin, 2002). Given that boards are social entities (Sonnenfeld,

TABLE 1.1
Characteristics of Healthy and Unhealthy Board Cultures

Healthy Boards Are Marked By	Unhealthy Boards Are Marked By
Distributed influence	Dominant inner circle
Collective wisdom	Individual convictions
Open-minded listeners	Closed-minded speakers
Constructive dissent	Back-channel agitation
Transparency	Opacity
Confidentiality	Seepage
Diligence	Disengagement
Respect and trust	Disregard and distrust
Clear expectations	Ambiguous expectations
Mutual accountability	Collective impunity

Note. Adapted from Chait, 2016, May/June, p. 22.

2002), they have sets of dynamics (created over time and taught to new-comers) that are best explained through the lens of organizational culture. "Most directors aren't aware of the group dynamics that affect the board's behavior . . . [and] how much their membership in groups influences their behavior and how others behave toward them" and are, therefore, "blind to the need to correct it in some cases or to exploit it in others" (Alderfer, 1986, p. 38).

As we discuss later, culture matters; how it manifests itself is likely different from board to board, leading to strengths that can be leveraged and potential vulnerabilities that should be minimized. What we do know is that some board cultures tend to be more constructive than others. Chait (2016) contrasted the hallmarks of effective and ineffective board cultures (see Table 1.1).

Board culture matters because it influences factors such as who speaks and who has the final word; what issues get traction and which do not; how board members treat each other and the administration; how decisions get made; and even issues such as beliefs about the fundamental role of the board as one of external critic protecting stakeholder interests or one of the board working in partnership with the administration (see chapter 10).

Returning to the three previous scenarios, a single approach to the question "How do boards develop themselves to shift their work to fit current and future priorities?" is likely insufficient. Instead, boards should consider all three elements and work across the interdependent set—structure, content, and culture. Integration matters and attending to one part of the equation without due attention to the other two may not help boards get to where they need to be. The subsequent chapters of this book address many of the component parts of this challenge. But first, we turn to a framework that many boards have found helpful.

The Past, Present, and Future of Board Work

Although much longer lists exist (Association of Governing Boards of Universities and Colleges, 2010), board responsibilities can be categorized into four primary areas (Chait, Ryan, & Taylor, 2005; Committee of University Chairs [CUC], 2014):

1. Stating, and revising, if necessary, the university's mission and purpose
2. Monitoring university performance, quality, and compliance and holding the administration accountable
3. Developing and safeguarding the institution's financial and physical resources while monitoring risk
4. Being the conduit between the institution and its environment; advocating on its behalf; defending the university; and working to minimize undue intervention

Chait and colleagues (2005) offered a new framework for thinking about board work through their "governance as leadership" model:

- The *fiduciary* work of boards ensures that boards are stewards of their universities and that the universities are compliant with laws and regulations, making progress advancing the mission of the institution and using resources appropriately.
- The *strategic* work of boards focuses on advancing the university's mission and priorities in a changing environment of threats and opportunities while accounting for institutional strengths and weaknesses.
- The *generative* work brings diverse trustee knowledge and wisdom to the challenges and opportunities facing the university to provide leadership in partnership with the CEO. This final type of engagement—generative—is especially important when the issue is

still ambiguous and open to interpretation (Trower, 2013). Trustees bring their sensemaking abilities to perceive and frame issues to the collective work of the board to help the institution think wisely about its long-term viability and vitality.

Some boards have found this framework difficult to adopt. A related (yet alternative) way that might be more easily understood and put into practice is to still think of board work in three areas, but to also think of the work as it relates to time—past, present, and future. Governance work is tied to the *past* through board oversight and stewardship roles, the *present* in the board's problem-solving role, and the *future* with the board serving as strategists about what might happen and possible steps to take and as long-term guardians of the mission.

The oversight work of boards looks back at past performance. How well did the institution do regarding budget or enrollment projections? How well is the investment strategy working? What have been the returns? Accountability and oversight are essential functions for boards. This work has the board looking in the rearview mirror.

Obviously, boards also work in the present, particularly related to their problem-solving role. Asking questions such as "What is the cost of the proposed new financial aid policy?" or "Are we confident that students are learning?" are tied to the present, as are issues like understanding institutional responses to sexual misconduct or student protests over diversity and inclusion. The present is where problems are solved and where questions surface regarding forthcoming decisions. This is the work of the board looking out the side windows.

Finally, boards must look well into the future. This is where the strategic and generative work is done. In this work, boards are not problem-solvers, but problem-seekers, working to find and frame issues for better understanding (Trower, 2013). This work is essential, yet too often overlooked by boards as they focus mostly on the past and present. As Sawyer (2007) noted, "The most transformative creativity results when a group either thinks of a new way to frame a problem or finds a new problem that no one noticed before" (p. 16). Asking questions about topics such as what demographic changes might mean for the university, how the economy is changing in ways to which the university might better respond, or what a new type of technology might mean for creating a competitive advantage helps focus boards on the future. This work has the board collectively looking out the windshield— over the horizon (or trying to see around corners).

Each point in time requires boards to adopt different ways of thinking. The more different ways boards can think in the boardroom the better. The accountability/oversight role is, fundamentally, *analytic*. What are the facts and what do they suggest? How do we evaluate the evidence? The problem-solving role requires an *inquisitive* perspective. Questions such as "What?" and "Why?" are inquisitive. The strategy/problem-finding role asks boards to be *exploratory* and get at the "So what?" questions like "What sense do we make of this or that?" and "What are the potential consequences of . . . ?" Table 1.2 summarizes these ideas regarding past, present, and future.

Boards can use this framework to review their performance, looking at both the allocation of time across the past, present, and future dimensions and at the board's capacity to do this different type of work (see Tables 1.3 and 1.4).

TABLE 1.2
Board Work: The Past, Present, and Future

	The Past	*The Present*	*The Future*
Function	Oversight of progress/ Accountability	Problem-solving	Strategy/ Problem-finding/ Mission guardian role
Mind-set	Analytic	Inquisitive	Exploratory
Sample questions boards ask	How did our actual performance compare with our budget projections? How well is our investment strategy working? Did the president have a successful year?	What is the cost of the new tuition and financial aid policy? Are we confident that students are learning? What are we doing about the academic performance of athletes?	What might X mean for our campus? What are the emerging trends in the economy to which we should respond?

TABLE 1.3
Board Percentage of Time Allocated to Past, Present, and Future (Current and Anticipated)

	The Past	*The Present*	*The Future*
	Oversight of progress Accountability	Problem-solving	Strategy Problem-seeking
Percentage of time we are currently spending	____ %	____ %	____ %
Percentage of time we anticipate needing to spend	____ %	____ %	____ %

TABLE 1.4
Past Performance GPA for the Three Types of Work

	Oversight of Progress Accountability (Mind-set: Analytic)	*Problem-Solving (Mind-set: Inquisitive)*	*Strategy Problem-Finding (Mind-set: Exploratory)*
Performance GPA			

Finally, boards can use this framework as a way to begin to assess their performance. The results, coupled with the allocation of time (current and anticipated) can be helpful for boards interested in intentionally using their time most effectively. For each element, have the trustees assign the board a letter grade (A, B, C, D, F) to their focus in considering the past, staying in the present, and looking to the future. By thinking about their work across these three domains, boards can begin to recognize where they are working well and where there are areas for improvement. That was the case for the three boards described at the beginning of this chapter.

Applying the Framework

The first board (in crisis mode) in the opening scenarios determined that nearly 80% of its time was spent on problem-solving. That board collectively recognized that it needed to move more work toward strategy and problem-finding. At the same time, it decided to develop a more consistent approach to oversight. The trustees were so busy solving problems that they neither looked backward to track institutional progress nor carved out time to look forward. Attention was only on the immediate. The board discussed how its recent oversight work was tied to crisis-driven issues and only tapped the most readily available data. The board was not intentional about its focus, so, as a practical step, it decided to develop a board-level dashboard on key metrics trustees felt were important (e.g., enrollment in undergraduate and graduate programs and the net tuition generated by programs). Regarding the future and strategy, the board decided to reconstitute a committee it once had on strategic planning and reframed the work away from planning to environmental scanning and trend analysis. The board is currently developing a structure and culture to engage deans and faculty leaders meaningfully in this committee's work that will focus on the college's 10- to 15-year future. The outcomes of the revised committee's work will then support campus planning efforts led by the president and faculty leaders.

The board in the second scenario decided that the past president had taken complete responsibility for the strategy and problem-finding work (future focus) as well as the problem-solving work (present focus). The board was left with oversight, work they determined was important but not interesting. "Many boards are ineffectual not just because they are confused about their role, but because they are dissatisfied with their role. They do not do their job well because their job does not strike them as worth doing well" (Chait et al., 2005, p. 16). A key contributor to board malaise is often that holding others accountable is a task not intrinsically rewarding. Chait and colleagues noted, "Who has ever been moved to join a board thinking, 'I really want to hold this organization to account?'" (p. 19). The participation (or lack of it) by this board was a case in point. The trustees wanted more from their engagement and sought to make meaningful contributions to the future trajectory of the institution.

The third board recognized that it was unbalanced in its approach across the different issues it discussed. It worked across all three areas—accountability, problem-solving, and strategy—but did so in ways that were uneven by topic. For example, the board felt it had an appropriate balance across all three domains with respect to the physical plant and the master planning issues. But the board determined that regarding other topics, it spent too much time on oversight and had not made the same types of substantive contributions as they had on campus infrastructure. It had work to do across all three domains, particularly when it came to the student experience and the state's completion goals. It could provide some oversight but didn't have the knowledge or skills to provide strategy or problem-solving related to students and their academic achievement. This conversation opened the door for the board to express to the president its desire to be more knowledgeable about these topics and how best they could gain such knowledge, and the board was able to say that the president could rely more heavily on his team's expertise to assist with board education.

Conclusion

Most boards do not struggle because they don't understand their roles and responsibilities. Instead, they may not recognize the ways in which their work has evolved and, in turn, change their ways of operating to add more value. They may look for structural changes without attention to the substance of their work or the impact of culture. "Boards that ignore a dysfunctional culture, abide the status quo, and focus on artifacts [structure for instance] rather than assumptions will pay a far steeper price: mediocre governance at best and abysmal performance at worse" (Chait, 2016, p. 24).

A comprehensive understanding of the intersection of structure, content, and culture and an intentional integration (e.g., aligning board size with committee-centric approaches to governance) will help boards operationalize their work across the three points in time of board work: the oversight/past, problem-solving/present, and problem-finding and strategy/future.

Questions for Boards

1. Has our board evolved its governance practices to keep pace with the times (and to ensure effectiveness given the institution's context)? What old habits do we still hold dear even though they are outdated?
2. Are we paying attention to and asking the right questions about board structure, content, and culture?
3. Are we spending appropriate amounts of time looking at the past (oversight), the present (problem-solving), and the future (problem-finding, strategy)?
4. What letter grades do we give ourselves (and what's our GPA) for effectiveness in each role—analytic (past), inquisitive (present), and exploratory (future)?

For Further Insight

To follow up on some of the issues raised in this chapter, we suggest:

- Chapter 5: Right Answers; Wrong Questions
- Chapter 6: Spending Scarce Time Wisely
- Chapter 9: The "Jobs" of Committees: Of Drill Bits and Milkshakes
- Chapter 10: The Culture of Boards: Making the Invisible Visible

---

2

THE "DAMNED IF YOU DO, DAMNED IF YOU DON'T" DYNAMICS OF GOVERNING

B oards find themselves facing difficult situations across a range of topics. The work of governance can be challenging, and some would argue
that the deck is stacked against boards being able to work effectively
and efficiently. Trustees are volunteers who attempt to bring their skills and
expertise developed and honed elsewhere to higher education. Furthermore,
boards meet infrequently; private university boards meet only three or four
times a year, and public boards do not meet much more frequently. Being a
trustee is a difficult volunteer role, and boards often find themselves facing
"damned if you do, damned if you don't" situations.

Not Easy Work

Governance is difficult, time-consuming work for volunteer trustees. Often,
and with seemingly increased frequency, the popular press has abounded
with stories about college and university governance gone awry. Regularly
accompanying the headlines are comments by readers that appear at the end
of the articles. We have all seen them: Some of those comments are well
formulated and advance the conversation about good governance, but unfortunately, many are misinformed or just plain nasty. They tend to be the ones
posted anonymously. Although the news stories give renewed attention to
the power and role of governance and call out some of the tensions, the comments accompanying those articles suggest that much more understanding
is needed about the role and function of lay boards of trustees, part of our
historical structure since America's earliest colonial colleges (see chapter 16
for a look at a colonial college's governance and its relevance for today).

A Difficult Job in Difficult Times

Governance can be arduous, as we will explain. Being a trustee is a difficult volunteer role, and boards often find themselves in "damned if you do, damned if you don't" situations. Amid the vitriol and mudslinging that occurs in the media as well as on campus around governance, our intent is not to play the metaphorical violin and feel sorry for trustees, but we do want to point out a few harsh realities with which today's boards must cope.

Responding to Tricky, If Not Impossible, Decisions Thrust Upon Them

Boards do not get to choose the issues that come before them. Some problems and quandaries that end up on board agendas can be anticipated—for example, student concerns (and in some places protests) regarding race and equity, difficult budget decisions, and choices about investing in new buildings or even new campuses. Yet, even if anticipated, the board never knows how an issue will play out in real time, and there often are no right answers or simple paths forward. For example, at one institution, while the board was engaged in a campus master plan approval process, the mayor of the city in which the university was located would not allow building permits to be granted until the university "took care of its parking problem." That problem, in effect, was the mayor's frustration with students parking in front of local businesses adjoining the campus. (Those parking spots were closer to the classrooms than on-campus parking.) Thus, a discussion that started as campus master planning, quickly (d)evolved into town-gown relationships, the role of the university in dealing with those issues, and the power of the mayor to hold the university hostage until it "solved" the parking problem in town.

Although this situation was resolved with the university moving the construction of a parking garage to its top priority, other more obstinate issues simply cannot be predicted. For example, from the not-so-distant past, it is not as if the boards in Louisiana planned for the $940-million budget deficit in 2016 (Wexler, 2016). Neither could Mount St. Mary's University's board anticipate the accreditation issues or other fallout from its (now former) president's remarks about students (including picking up the pieces after his resignation) (Jaschik, 2016). Recall also the University of Missouri's Board of Curators in 2015 dealing with the actions of a faculty member, acting on her own accord and captured on video, related to the racial and ethnic protests taking place on campus, that resulted in criminal charges against her and, ultimately, the termination of her employment (Addo, 2016).

Balancing Both Immediate and Long-Term Concerns and Dealing With Complex Issues

Taking the long view sometimes seems nearly impossible in a culture obsessed with speed and desirous of instant gratification. First, the 24-hour news cycle, but more importantly the constant buzz of social media, means that boards and institutional leaders need to constantly attend to the immediate. And one poor choice (i.e., tweet) by a trustee or a campus representative can create a scramble to control a situation or at least limit damage.

Second, the complexity of academic institutions coupled with situational urgency often means that a short-term focus easily becomes the default. Taking the long-term view is difficult for a host of reasons including (a) students—on campus for only a short time (in the scheme of things)—who are not timid about issuing immediate demands for fast action, regardless of well-laid plans and institutional priorities; (b) four generations of faculty, often with competing interests, who have seen their jobs change a great deal over the years (including increased expectations for research, teaching, and service), expecting different things from the university (in terms of support and consultation) on different timetables (which usually means now); and (c) administrators who must grapple with "crises" on a nearly daily basis. The urgent all too often pushes out the important. These factors combine so that boards find themselves at once caught up in the demands of the immediate while needing to never lose sight of the long term. But, as Harvard sociologist David Reisman reportedly said, the role of boards is to "protect the future from the present" (Bowen & Tobin, 2015, p. 138).

Boards have three fundamental responsibilities (Association of Governing Boards of Universities and Colleges, 2015a) that require them to balance the needs of today with those of the future.

1. Duty of Care (competence and diligence): the care that an ordinarily prudent person would exercise in a like position and under similar circumstances. Trustees have the duty to exercise reasonable care when making decisions as stewards of the institution—to actively participate in organizational planning and decision-making and to make sound and informed judgments.
2. Duty of Loyalty (fidelity): the undivided allegiance board members must give when making decisions. Board members may not use information obtained as a member for personal gain and must act in the best interests of the institution. When acting on behalf of the institution, board members must put institutional interests before any personal or professional concerns and avoid potential conflicts of interest.

3. Duty of Obedience (staying true to mission): the requirement for board members not to act in a way inconsistent with the central goals—the mission—of the institution. A basis for this rule lies in the public's trust that the institution will oversee assets (financial, physical, and otherwise) to fulfill its mission. Board members must ensure that the institution complies with all applicable federal, state, and local laws and regulations.

Although it is hoped that all individual members of the campus community would act in such ways, no other group has the same legal and ethical requirement to do so. Board members are not employees and have a fundamentally different relationship with the college, university, or state system.

Deciding in the Spotlight

Boards are governing in difficult times of heightened scrutiny; in fact, public boards need to govern in front of the public. Imagine trying to have a thoughtful, candid, difficult conversation about controversial issues with your spouse or entire family surrounded by invested onlookers—and then covered by the press to boot. This is the experience of public boards.

For instance, we would bet that most, if not all, boards should be seriously grappling with how to best deal with the long-term financial health of their institutions. Even well-endowed institutions face economic issues and, sometimes, budget shortfalls. In January 2013, Moody's (2013) downgraded the entire American higher education sector to negative, and that outlook continued for 2014 (Troop, 2014). In 2015, Moody's revised its assessment from negative to stable (Moody's, 2015) which lasted for the boom years of 2016 and 2017, but things went south again for 2018 (A. Harris, 2017). As one trustee said in a personal interview, "We have a relatively undercapitalized institution, offering a largely undifferentiated product, in an increasingly price-sensitive market, characterized by declining demographics." Who would be bullish on that? How can boards explore complex and contentious issues, engage in dialogue, or ponder and wonder aloud on difficult and complex issues such as the institution's financial well-being when the news media may cover their every thought? The point that follows is related.

Balancing Competing Interests

Because the board needs to take the long view (but also provide counsel and make decisions regarding immediate challenges) and because of its duties of care, loyalty, and obedience, it must try to balance the competing interests of a range of stakeholders. Stakeholders include, among others, faculty from multiple disciplines, staff members, current and future students, alumni, community and civic groups, neighborhood associations, policymakers, and boosters. Unlike corporate settings where a common and clear set of metrics can guide decision-making (e.g., maximizing shareholder return), higher education has a messy set of contradictory metrics, each with their own advocates and supporters. Does a university prioritize undergraduate or graduate education? Advance basic research or support professional schools and practical application? Invest in more parking or environmental sustainability? The answer facing most administrators and boards is yes to all.

In addition to long-term versus short-term views, on all campuses, other paradoxical issues are at hand. Should the board drive change or work to help maintain stability? Focus on core competencies or new ones? Save and build the endowment or innovate and invest? And in the meantime, the public (including students and their families) wants everything better, cheaper, and faster. Every single decision a board makes is going to please some and upset others. That's reality.

Acting as a Group

We all know how difficult it is to make certain decisions alone, right? Although some college and university boards are small, the average size of private university boards is 29 (Association of Governing Boards of Universities and Colleges, 2016). As a *collective,* boards must deliberate issues, hear all sides, seek optimal solutions, and come to decisions that will be made public. Imagine *you* have to come to a mutually acceptable decision with competing interests, fast, in a group, and under the spotlight (and by the way, with interim leadership, as is often the case). We think we can all agree: This is a tough job. (We explore the dynamics of group decision-making throughout the rest of the book, especially chapters 8–11.)

Dealing With the Challenges of Accountability

Board work is difficult because it lacks natural systems of accountability. Who is watching the board, and to what extent does the board see itself as accountable? And for what? Boards work well when they take their own accountability seriously, but too often they do not. Yes, the faculty can vote no confidence in the board, and the state attorney general can intervene, as in the fairly recent case at Cooper Union (E. Harris, 2015) and the historic case at Adelphi University (Gearty, 1998). But for the most part, boards must develop the ability and conscientiousness to establish their own mechanisms for accountability (see chapter 7 for a more comprehensive discussion on ensuring accountability).

Addressing Unfamiliar Issues

Often trustees need to make decisions on unfamiliar issues. Some issues, although not completely unique to higher education, simply are not that common in trustees' daily lives—granting or revoking tenure, making decisions on potentially controversial honorary degree recipients (or revoking those degrees awarded by their predecessors; e.g., Michigan State and former Zimbabwe president Robert Mugabe [AP, 2008]; The Ohio State University and Bill Cosby [AP, 2018]), signing off on faculty handbooks, and understanding fund accounting or the concept of tuition discounting (tell us again why we charge our "customers" less than it costs to produce our "product"). Individual trustees may have few reservoirs of experience to draw upon for some of the decisions that make their way to the boardroom.

Where Good Governance Reigns

Finally, we must not forget that board members are volunteers, a preponderance of whom are members of the general public and not of the academy. Board members are appointed (public boards or by some sponsoring orders at some private boards), elected (variously by alumni, faculty, or students, or in general elections in some states), or asked to volunteer. Most college and university boards are composed of influential individuals who care deeply about the institutions they serve. It's true that some come with an agenda, but, by and large, that's not the case (other than to improve the institutions or state systems they govern). Trustees want to do good work, and they want their institutions to thrive. These volunteer boards can and do add value to the institutions they govern by bringing collective expertise, insight, and wisdom.

Effective boards share some important ways of thinking about governance:

- Recognizing that the stakes are high, and have perhaps never been higher, for the institutions they serve
- Realizing that all trustees and boards have room to improve—and making a commitment to seeking feedback, reviewing their work, learning, and making changes
- Having a certain "positive restlessness" that keeps them always striving to do better (Kuh, Kinzie, Schuh, & Whitt, 2005, p. 46)
- Being self-aware and thinking about their collective impact while keeping cognizant of complexity and the paradoxes surrounding them
- Paying attention to substance, structure, culture, process, and boardroom dynamics

- Maintaining the ability to adapt to changing circumstances and pivot rather than getting trapped in stale routines (however comfortable they may be)

We talk about these issues and others throughout the remainder of this book.

Recommendations for Boards

This chapter is not an apologist's perspective on governance today. Given the complexity of the world in which boards must govern, we realize that we run the risk of ridicule for oversimplifying and making broad-brush statements (and if this book had an online comments section like the news articles we have cited previously, we'd fully expect some cynical reactions). We also realize that there are no panaceas, no right answers, and no silver bullet solutions to governance; instead, we offer here and throughout this book different ways for boards to think about and approach the situations they encounter. Here we offer six ideas boards might consider to help ensure that they are ready when (not if) messy issues arise.

1. With the administration, and within the parameters set forth by the institution's bylaws, develop an explicit understanding of good governance. This requires focused discussion (and likely more than one conversation) that clarifies otherwise unstated assumptions across individual board members and an explicit agreement about the work of individual trustees and the work of the board (as a board and in committees). We have seen boards write "job descriptions" for trustees. Importantly, the board's governance "job" should be communicated to the faculty. Faculty too often do not understand the work of boards or what it requires of these volunteers (and thus this chapter). Relaying that to faculty leaders can be helpful.
2. Practice ("scrimmage"), when times are good, on easier issues. Boards cannot predict what difficult issues will surface and must be well practiced to take on the most unexpected challenges. Every board meeting, when the institution is not in a crisis, is an opportunity for the board to take a "deep dive" into an important issue. For example, in 2014, the Baylor University Board of Regents spent a portion of its July retreat on two big issues: (a) image and brand and (b) enrollment management. They learned how to have constructive dialogue and debate, because not all regents agreed on what the image was and should be, what the "brand" was or should be, or had knowledge of how the admission's office goes

about its business. Regents had to "score" the disguised profiles of eight prospective students and decide whether to admit, deny, or defer and, if admit, what financial aid package to provide. These scrimmages, if you will, helped the board govern better when the university later faced issues around sexual misconduct, athletics, and the presidency (Watkins, 2016).

3. Review cases in the news and ask, "What can we learn? What if that were us?" Numerous boards have used well-publicized cases to, in essence, scrimmage. A few well-known cases exist, with plenty of news coverage and institutional documentation to allow the board opportunities to "practice," including the University of Virginia's firing and subsequent rehiring of President Teresa Sullivan (Stripling, 2012); Penn State's football coach scandal (Hobson, 2017); Michigan State's sexual assault cases (Jenkins, 2018; Miller, 2018); Middlebury's free speech issues (Beinart, 2017); and Dartmouth College's fraternity woes (Rocheleau, 2015).

4. Consider the perspectives of multiple stakeholders by asking, "Who are the stakeholders for this decision? What's at stake for them, particularly the faculty and students? Why?" Engage in stakeholder mapping. Ask "What is the likely dominant perspective from each group? What likely influences their view? What does the board need to know to make a wise and informed decision (and anticipate fallout, both supportive and critical)?"

5. When appropriate, seek input from key stakeholders, being especially cognizant of your institution's shared governance expectations (see chapter 15 on shared governance). Almost every decision boards ponder affects the faculty, some more directly than others. Issues of curriculum, online courses, new majors, the discontinuation of majors or departmental closure—all must involve the faculty in some fashion. In the previously mentioned University of Virginia case, it was the faculty who led the opposition to President Sullivan's firing and the faculty who ensured that she was reinstated. Boards are well advised to never underestimate the faculty. In other cases, the alumni or students form powerful coalitions. At Baylor, in 2017, it was two megadonors who demanded major changes in the wake of the sexual assault scandal. In 2017, two conservative University of California, Berkeley student groups sued the institution over a planned appearance by right-wing political commentator Ann Coulter that was ultimately canceled (Cone, 2017).

6. Communicate not only the decision outcomes but also the deliberations. Help those affected stakeholders understand the different viewpoints that were broached in the boardroom in addition to the outcomes of the deliberation.

Conclusion

Boards will likely face "damned if you do, damned if you don't" scenarios for the foreseeable future. The better prepared boards are to address the big challenges ahead, the better our institutions will be. The discussion in this chapter shows that boards cannot control all of the factors that shape the governance milieu and they must play with the hand they are dealt; however, we've outlined here practical steps boards can take to mitigate some factors that make governance especially challenging. All of this said, boards themselves sometimes contribute to "damned if you do" situations (we address such behaviors throughout this book, particularly in the next chapter on mediocrity). Thus, the challenges of governing are nothing less than structural, contextual, and self-inflicted, and sometimes a combination of all three.

Questions for Boards

1. What are the factors that hinder more effective governance at your institution? To what extent can the board influence those factors?
2. Boards often face competing interests. What are they at your institution? How, and how well, does the board handle those competing interests?
3. What are the expectations for individual trustees? How much consensus is there among the board related to these expectations? How are they communicated and assessed?
4. How often does the board step back from its work to reflect on how well it is governing?
5. How can it make these conversations part of its regular work?

For Further Insight

To follow up on some of the issues raised in this chapter, we suggest:

- Chapter 3: Is Your Board Mediocre?
- Chapter 4: Individual Competencies for Collective Impact
- Chapter 10: The Culture of Boards: Making the Invisible Visible
- Chapter 13: Creating the Capacity for Trying Issues
- Chapter 15: Getting to Grips With Shared Governance
- Chapter 16: Governing Circa 1749

3

IS YOUR BOARD MEDIOCRE?

arvard Business School professor Dutch Leonard (2013) said, "The central challenge for nonprofit leadership is that mediocrity is survivable." His observation—sad but true—may apply to some college and university governing boards. However, given the challenges facing higher education today, mediocrity might not be survivable. A key thread of a conversation at a recent conference of presidents concerned the dangers of mediocre governance. The higher education and popular press are replete with stories not only of underwhelming board performance (e.g., Sweet Briar [Casteen, 2015] and the University of Texas at Austin [Marcus, 2015] but also of governance gone awry, like Penn State [Hobson, 2017], University of Virginia [Stripling, 2012], South Carolina State [Knich & Smith, 2012], and Suffolk University [Jaschik, 2016]). Regardless of whether the board caused the headlines for poor performance, a certain truth has surfaced about some college and university boards—they are minimally sufficient. This chapter discusses what lies behind mediocrity and how boards can move beyond it.

Mired in Mediocrity

When conducting board assessments, we like to ask trustees to provide a letter grade to their board's overall performance. On average, trustees give their boards a C+ grade. And when we ask why they give this grade, trustees say such things as the following:

- "We're a good, but not great, board."
- "I've been on worse boards."
- "I suspect we're better in our own minds than in the minds of the senior staff."
- "We never discuss our performance; our focus is on the administration's performance."

- "We love this institution, but I'm not sure we really know how to govern well."

These are not particularly encouraging responses. In chapter 2, we explored elements of the context of governance that prove challenging. Here we focus on what boards do to themselves that impedes effective governance.

Why Do Some College and University Boards Underperform?

The boards in the headlines are often those that are dysfunctional (think Adelphi University, Suffolk University, or the University of Virginia, or whatever boards were in the news this past month). Although these boards may well deserve their negative spotlight, most boards are *not* dysfunctional like those in the headlines—they simply can do more to be an asset to the institutions they govern. Boards do not add as much value as they should for many reasons; some of the more common ones we've seen are discussed in the following sections.

The Focus Is on the "Pretty Ponies"

One trustee we know remarked, "Our board meetings are dog-and-pony shows, but the administration only trots out the pretty ponies." If all the trustees hear is how great everything is going, they tend to assume that everything really is great, and they may become complacent. "A good board is a quiet board" goes this line of reasoning. If the administration keeps the board busy listening to reports and attending to mostly (or only) the positive, boards cannot live up to their potential. Passive listening leads to passive engagement and mediocre governance. Trustees do not gain the knowledge or practice to ask insightful questions or add perspectives that the administration will find helpful.

The "Done" Decisions

Similarly, too often boards only learn about issues after they have already been decided, either by an overly powerful executive committee or the administration. Such a practice, once exposed, quickly becomes irksome. Trustees, particularly those who are accomplished individuals, have little time and patience to rehash old decisions or to be rubber stamps for others who think they know better. Their patience wears thin hearing long reports and then learning that a decision has been made that is difficult to revisit.

Brainpower Goes Untapped

Too often trustees do not bring their "A game" when it comes to board work. In some instances, the administration does not involve the board in important and meaty matters. And other times, trustees do not do their homework prior to meetings that would allow them to engage fully. Regardless of cause, when trustees check out mentally, they provide no value. That can lead to apathy that not only affects the board's performance at meetings but also can result in lackluster philanthropic support. Furthermore, if the right people are on the board, the institution is missing a key opportunity for their input.

The One-Issue Trustee Reigns

At a board with which one of us worked, the answer to every institutional problem was "women's golf." They didn't have a team, and one trustee clearly wanted one. The institution needed to increase enrollment and brought that issue to the board. "Invest in women's golf" came the solution from one of the most vocal trustees. The institution wanted to engage alumni more effectively. "Women's golf," that same trustee urged a few hours later in the meeting, speculating, "Women golfers will be dedicated alumnae." During discussions about increasing auxiliary revenue, he jumped in with "Well, you know, we should consider improving the golf course and creating a women's golf team." And so it goes. The board and the president didn't have the skill or will to rein in this trustee and his sole solution.

Congeniality Is Not Collegiality

Many boards suffer from being overly polite and deferential—both of which result in mediocrity. In contrast, the best colleagues take each other on, pushing each other's thinking and debating ideas, all with the focus of advancing the common good (and not simply grandstanding). High-performing boards do not shy away from difficult conversations and conflicting views and ideas. Instead, they understand that such messy, even uncomfortable, dialogues are essential to understanding complex issues and eventually lead to better decisions. And at the end of the day (or board meeting), those trustees are able to put aside their differences and move ahead.

Good (Enough) Is the Enemy of Great

Too often we hear that the board is pretty good—in fact, good enough or "better than we used to be." Why push harder for more? This situation is all too common. Many boards believe that behaviors that worked sufficiently in the past will continue to serve the board and the institution today and into the future. But given the increasing and changing demands on higher education institutions and their leaders, governance that was once good enough no longer is. They hold outdated metrics of board performance such as whether trustees attend board meetings from start to finish or whether they contribute financially.

Part of the challenge is that many boards do not take the time to assess themselves or their meetings meaningfully. And those boards that do ask questions of themselves rarely yield constructive insights. Instead, trustees make comments such as "I liked the pace of the meeting" or "We had good attendance" without getting to what really matters such as whether all trustees were meaningfully engaged, whether trustees named the elephant in the room, whether underlying feelings preventing movement were vetted appropriately, or whether trustees debated issues rather than simply moving straight to consensus and voting.

Boards Don't Know Otherwise

Unlike administrators and faculty who have deep and extensive professional networks to help them not only find solutions to problems but also provide a set of benchmarks, most trustees have neither as they rarely interact with trustees from other boards. Trustees tend not to know individuals who serve on other university or college boards. They operate in isolation without ready benchmarks of performance or a network of trustees to engage. The result is that most trustees assume that as their board goes, so go all other boards. This is clearly not the case. Too often boards look only to their own histories and practices as a guide for the future rather than looking at other (high-performing) boards.

Presidents Perpetuate the Problem

There are four reasons presidents do not lead boards from mediocrity. First, some presidents simply believe that boards do not have the knowledge to help in meaningful ways. And depending on who sits on the board, this unfortunately may be true. Second, once trustees are invited in, they'll never get out of the details. The potential risks to management aren't worth the rewards of engaged boards. Third, presidents may not believe they have the requisite time to devote to governance. The demands on their time are great, and a board that is good enough (rather than great) allows for presidential time to be spent elsewhere. Finally, presidents simply are inexperienced working effectively with boards. A national study of presidents summarized in the Association of Governing Boards of Universities and Colleges' (AGB's) magazine *Trusteeship* found that approximately 25% of presidents had no experience working with boards prior to ascending to the presidency (Eckel, 2013). This meant they had not even staffed committees; thus, their first experience with governance up close is from the presidential seat.

Governance Structure Contributes

Mediocrity in the boardroom is sometimes not because of what boards do but because of the structures through which they operate. Boards get mired in mediocrity related to the work and structure of governance for three primary reasons. First, board work is episodic—with infrequent meetings—and boards do not benefit from repetition and practice or from an easy continuity between meetings. Boards do not gain the skill and knowledge that comes with frequent repetition. In many ways, this is akin to a runner only lacing up for 10k races and not running between races. The governance muscle loses any memory it developed, if it developed any at all.

Second, on many boards, the executive committee has undue influence. That imbalance of influence may cause the rest of the group to check out, leaving a lot of complex work in the hands of too few trustees. We talk more about this phenomenon in chapter 10 (on culture) and chapter 11 (on power and influence). Importantly, boards with an imbalance in power seem to underperform in both the short and long terms. They may gain efficiency but lose effectiveness.

Third, the mind-set of what constitutes effective trusteeship matters. Some trustees believe that they serve on the board to be decisive—to make decisions. This singlemindedness does not take advantage of all that boards can offer. It shortchanges the role of boards in exploring and understanding issues and their complexity, rushes decision-making, and likely excludes some quieter trustees who first seek to understand before rushing to judgment.

Boards Are Underconfident or Overconfident

The right level of confidence matters in boardrooms, but some boards are underconfident and others overly so. Both are problematic. Underconfident boards don't live up to expectations. They are wary of asking questions or probing the issues, skittish about holding the president accountable, and ambivalent about their own accountability. Underconfidence can occur when trustees lack familiarity with higher education, its nuances and culture, and when trustees only engage periodically (as previously mentioned). Underconfidence leads to "light touch" trusteeship, which often adds little value (although trustees enjoy the meals, camaraderie, and time spent on campus).

Overconfidence has its own problems. Arrogant boards can't seem to listen; they are too busy talking, if not directing. They believe that their lessons and skills, typically from the private sector, will automatically translate well into higher education. As McFarlan (1999) noted, "Even the best intentions can prove disastrous when new board members fail to understand that their traditional business experience can carry them only so far" (p. 65) in the nonprofit world. In fact, "almost none of what is learned through service on a corporate board is true of non-profit board work" (p. 76). Also, as Bowen (1994) stated, "Board members with no visceral feel for an organization may bring values to the table that are simply inappropriate" (p. 41). Thus, an overconfident board—heralding from any sector—can result in a so-called all answers, no questions board. Overconfidence may be driven by ego (and the larger the individual egos, the more overconfident the board can be collectively) or it can stem from the lack of understanding of the realities of higher education—its culture, financial model, and ways of working. Either way, overconfidence leads to mediocrity (if not worse).

Out of the Quagmire of Mediocrity

We have seen a continued increase in the number of boards that acknowledge that they can and should govern better. To do this they must (a) recognize their mediocrity (no small feat), or at least become aware that they can govern better; (b) have the will and desire to improve; and (c) chart a path forward. What follows are strategies that have proven successful for many boards with which we have worked.

Look in the Mirror

The first step on the pathway to improvement is recognition. Boards must focus attention on themselves and how they govern. For many reasons, some boards do not address their own performance in a systematic and productive way. First, boards are composed of volunteers who may not see themselves as sufficiently knowledgeable about governance or feel they lack the expertise to evaluate themselves. Second, boards pressed for time don't stop to question their performance. They figure "leave well enough alone." Third, some boards may not think the effort will lead to any substantive changes. "We have operated this way for years (decades) and will likely continue to do so. We tried to make a change once, but it didn't work." A fourth reason is that it might not even occur to the trustees that they should evaluate themselves; they have no history of doing so. These boards feel that their job is to evaluate the president, not themselves. Finally, there is no precipitating event. A negative news story about the institution or a board can jar a board to action. But most boards, particularly mediocre ones, remain out of the media spotlight. Without a push, inertia prevails. Without looking in the metaphorical mirror, they're stuck where they are.

Gather Some Data and Do Something With It

Boards expect their institutions to make decisions based on data; they should do the same. Ask trustees in a systematic way about their experiences serving on the board. This can be done using short and simple surveys or full-blown assessments, internally or with outside experts. (More ideas about board assessment will be provided later in the chapter.) The key is to discuss the results of the data and act upon them. Here is a simple strategy to get started: Ask board members to (anonymously) provide a letter grade for the board's overall performance. Calculate the GPA and display the range. Then ask, "If you could only do one thing to improve that grade, what would it be?" You can also ask, "What do you find most fulfilling about serving on this board?" and "What do you find most frustrating?"—again, anonymously, so people can be forthright. Discuss what trustees say and ways to build on what's fulfilling and fix what's frustrating. Ask, "What would success look like? How might we close the gaps between where we are now and where we want to be?"

Talk About Governance Expectations

Boards can benefit tremendously by talking not about their committee structures and the number and length of meetings, but about the expectations in the boardroom that guide their work. How well does the board value participation, preparation, transparency, teamwork, and accountability? What are the important and often unstated values that should shape their governance work? How closely do they match reality? Too often boards say they value participation but have a history of barely making a quorum. A good practice is to create a "Statement of Mutual Expectations" for serving on the board—what the institution can expect from trustees, what trustees can expect from the institution, and what trustees can expect from one another. Such a statement may include trustee guidelines for comportment, attendance, philanthropy, confidentiality, and institutional commitment to ensuring appropriate and timely information; transparency about critical incidents on campus; the student and faculty experience; and financial documentation.

Intellectually Engage the Brains

A goal of all boards is to tap the collective brainpower sitting around the table. Those brains are best engaged when the work is intellectually challenging (which might not often enough be the case). As Trower (2015) wrote in *Trusteeship*, "Send trustees a reading or two along with questions they should think about as they read. This way, trustees arrive at the meeting having done some critical thinking and prepared to discuss matters appropriately and thoughtfully" (p. 27). That work requires presidents and board leaders to think hard about the agenda and its content to ensure its relevance and level of engagement. The questions must be important and require thought. Good questions to go along with reading materials and reports might include the following: About what are you most optimistic? What has you most concerned? Are there essential elements of the issue not addressed in the reading? What assumptions underlie the reading's conclusions? Good questions posed in advance (a) keep the focus on what matters most, (b) help trustees think critically, and (c) help trustees add value as thought partners with the administration (for more, see chapter 6 on spending time wisely). Thinking up questions to go along with readings is a good task for either committee chairs or members of the governance committee.

Develop Governance Experiments

Although boards share much in common, they also vary tremendously in size, structure, and, more importantly, cultures, as we discuss later in chapter 10. Thus, boards should experiment with what practices work best for them given their current contexts and agendas. For example, increase the number and frequency of joint committee meetings on key topics (e.g., enrollment and finance or academic affairs and facilities or technology). Develop new task forces on emerging strategic challenges or opportunities and invite non-trustees to participate. Start *and* end each session with an executive session to put key issues on the table. Disallow all committee reports and instead have people read reports or meeting summaries prior to the start of the board meeting. Set up the boardroom with round tables that seat six to eight trustees each instead of a huge table that doesn't allow good line of sight. In some instances, these strategies work well; in other situations, they don't. The idea is to try something, test something, and evaluate it; try something else and test and evaluate that, too. Figure out what works for *your* board.

Ensure That Board Leaders Lead

Presidents can contribute to mediocrity when they believe they do not have the time to invest in board improvement. Sometimes this happens when presidents feel they need to lead both the institution and the board, because board leaders are overcommitted or don't understand their own leadership roles. Presidents cannot fulfill both roles effectively for very long. Board leaders need to demonstrate that they can and will lead the board and invest the time in doing so. Effective board leadership, particularly the chair, is essential to progress.

Create Continuity and Bridges Between Meetings

Board performance is affected mightily by the episodic nature of board meetings. For many private institutions, trustees show up on campus three times a year to "govern," too often with little institutional contact in between. A good practice is for the board chair, committee chair, or administrator who is in front of the board to remind trustees of what happened at the last meeting and inform them of what has happened since. Then toward the end of the meeting, the board chair should take a few minutes to summarize what happened (and ask, "Did I get that right?"), discuss implications, and say what will happen (what trustees can expect) next.

Boards that add value continue to evolve (a key point in chapter 1). They grow tired of the status quo. They understand that governance as usual will not help propel forward the institutions they serve. Those mired in mediocrity too often are satisfied and fall far short of effectiveness. Boards should develop a "positive restlessness" (Kuh et al., 2005, p. 46)—never quite satisfied with their performance. After all, the world is complex and ever-changing. Like the institutions they serve, boards must ask questions, learn from experience, adapt to changing conditions, and continually improve.

Assess the Board and Its Impact

Depending on the board and its level of sophistication, boards should develop regular and ongoing assessments; we outline two here.

First, certain fundamentals support good governance, and most boards should already have these in place. But some boards lack these elements and, without a firm foundation, will struggle to address future challenges. The board chair and institutional president should easily be able to answer the following questions, intended to help a board determine a baseline of its effectiveness:

- Do board members have a shared understanding of effective board governance?
- Do board members understand the meaning of shared governance at their institution, including who has authority and responsibility for what?
- Are there written expectations for trustees?
- Are there mechanisms for orienting and onboarding new board members?
- To thoughtfully contribute to the discourse, are board members asked to prepare for board meetings? (e.g., are key materials sent out 10 to 14 days in advance of meetings?) Do board members show up prepared for meetings?

- Do board members physically attend all meetings, with rare exceptions? How many call in? And how many simply don't show up? Are there consequences for not participating?
- Is it possible to tell what is most important for the institution by looking at the board agenda?
- Does the board have a clear meeting agenda, and is it designed to promote discussion and debate about the most pressing issues?
- Has the board (or a board subcommittee) reviewed the board bylaws within the last five years?

Second, boards need to know where they are performing well, where they have blind spots, and where they might need to improve. As they discuss their ability to navigate the whitewater ahead, boards may wish to consider the following:

- Time spent on meaningful issues. There are many complex issues to address and time is limited, so a board must spend it effectively and efficiently. Does the board have clear goals and objectives for each meeting? (See chapter 6 for more about spending time effectively.) To what extent do discussions allow the board to explore complicated topics? Is the meeting efficient? Does the board take the necessary time to deliberate on important issues?
- Appropriate data and information. Does the board have the information it needs to govern well? What qualitative and quantitative data are essential for all board members to have prior to the meeting?
- The use of board member talent and knowledge. Board members should be intentionally selected or invited to participate based on their talents, skill sets, knowledge, and ability to work well together. To what extent is the board composed of diverse thinkers? Are the areas of expertise that the institution needs reflected in the various members of the board? How well does the board tap into the collective wisdom of its members? Does the board work together as a high-performing team? Does the board add value?
- The relationship between the board and the president. The board-president relationship is complex, in part because of the multiple roles involved: The board oversees the president as boss, serves as a strategic thought partner, and is also a coach. Does the board play these three roles well, or is it predisposed to one role over the others? Does the board regularly and effectively evaluate the president? Does the board listen to the president? Is there mutual trust, respect, and accountability? Is there open, two-way communication and

transparency? (See chapter 12 on board-president relationships for more.)

- Board integrity. The board should evaluate its sense of integrity as well as that of the president and college, university, or system. Does the board have the capacity to ensure that both it and the institution or system it oversees are operating within the boundaries of applicable laws? Does the board have and uphold a conflict-of-interest policy? How transparent is the board in its decision-making? Does the board maintain confidentiality?
- Board member satisfaction. It is important to understand the extent to which board members believe their work has a positive impact, their level of overall satisfaction with the board, and the degree to which they find the experience rewarding. After all, these roles are voluntary. And boards want to ensure they are getting the most from their volunteers.

Other categories of possible assessment include the participation and engagement of board members, the effectiveness of board education, and the depth of board knowledge. Furthermore, boards can assess performance in several ways. One approach is to look at simple yet potentially powerful questions as presented in a two-by-two matrix (see Figure 3.1) defined by frequency and value or impact. (Don't spend much time in that bottom right quadrant.)

Figure 3.1. Simple evaluation matrix: Frequency and value-added.

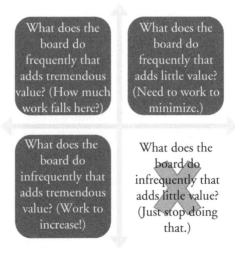

Conclusion

It seems that too many boards are stuck in or striving for mediocrity. While mediocrity is not the stated goal, actions suggest this is where the board is heading. Boards can get out of the quagmire of mediocrity and add value by being intentional in their work, membership, and use of time. Boards form habits and those habits become entrenched and unexamined. The objective of this chapter is to help boards, even those boards that think they are performing fine, reexamine their processes and ways of working. We use the terms *mediocre* and *mediocrity* intentionally. Most boards are not problematic; they simply are not fulfilling their potential.

Questions for Boards

1. Where would we place our board on a scale of 1 to 10 with 1 being mediocre and 10 being high performing? What accounts for that score? Do other board members agree with that assessment?
2. How high are our collective expectations for the board? Are we aiming too low?
3. What steps can we take to ensure that trustees are productively engaged at board meetings?
4. What do we need from the administration and what do we need from board leadership to ensure the board performs at its best?

For Further Insight

To follow up on some of the issues raised in this chapter, we suggest:

- Chapter 2: The "Damned If You Do, Damned If You Don't" Dynamics of Governing
- Chapter 4: Individual Competencies for Collective Impact
- Chapter 6: Spending Scarce Time Wisely
- Chapter 10: The Culture of Boards: Making the Invisible Visible
- Chapter 11: The (Not So) Hidden Dynamics of Power and Influence
- Chapter 13: Creating the Capacity for Trying Issues

4

INDIVIDUAL COMPETENCIES
FOR COLLECTIVE IMPACT

Much conversation about effective governance is about what boards do as a group, and that's fine, but, as collectives of individuals, the best boards are those where the sum adds up to more than the individual parts. We don't, however, choose a *group* of people for board service; we choose *individuals*. What are, and should be, the competencies of those individuals? In this chapter, we discuss the individual competencies of board members that will help improve how the collective governs.

A Collection of Individuals

Individuals matter to boards. It is a board's collective action that leads to effective governance, but the collective is only as good as the contributions made by individuals. Whereas the trustees of public colleges and universities or state systems are usually gubernatorial appointees, private or independent institutions are typically populated in self-perpetuating fashion, nominated by current board members. Some college and university boards have constituent representatives—for example, students, faculty, members of a religious order, alumni—and therefore accept nominations made by others.

Whatever the selection process, people join boards for a host of reasons and with a wide variety of backgrounds, skill sets, and expertise. In addition, trustees' expectations for board service vary a great deal. Some trustees have never served on a nonprofit board, let alone that of an academic institution. Others have corporate board experience and may lack knowledge of higher education and shared governance (discussed in chapter 15). Some trustees serve to "give back," whereas others are more personally motivated (looks good on a résumé) or have political reasons, or a combination of these.

The point is that most trustees come to the boardroom with no formal training about board service, scant insight about what to expect, and little understanding of what's expected of them—thus, the importance of a comprehensive orientation for new trustees. Too often orientations, if done at all, are quick and incomplete (and include a campus tour and lunch with a student or two). Effective orientations should provide an overview of the university or system, including budget, risk, mission, and values; bring new trustees up to speed on the external environment and the context in which they must govern; and finally, orient newcomers to how the board governs, the board's culture (see chapter 10), and what it means to be an effective trustee. Unfortunately, this last element is often overlooked—and with consequences. Table 4.1 provides an overview of what boards might consider as part of new trustee orientation. It's a long list, but trusteeship is a complex job. (And we suggest addressing these issues over time, not all in one sitting.)

TABLE 4.1
What to Include in New Trustee Orientation

The Institution Itself	Institutional Context	The Board Itself
Overview of the university and its key history	State or regional economy and economic needs	Board structure, committees
Institutional structure, administration, and faculty governance mechanisms	Relationship with state system/sponsoring order (if applicable)	Board members and board leaders
Academic offerings and research focus (if relevant)	Employer/graduate school expectations for graduates	Board culture and ways of working
Enrollment figures and trends, student profile	Accreditation— regional and specialized	Voting and decision-making processes
Institutional budgets, finances, and business model	Relevant state and federal regulations and policies/laws	Trustee expectations (attendance, preparation, philanthropy, engagement at and in between board meetings)
Student and faculty leaders	Potential student markets	Committee work
Physical plant and technological infrastructure	Competitors/peers	The social dynamics and expectations of the board

Avoiding That One Bad Apple

We hear many stories about boards and governance gone awry, and often about a "rogue" trustee—someone who doesn't understand the practice of governance or disruptively violates the culture of the board. Although boards and presidents hope they never have a rogue in their midst, a small study of community college presidents reported that 97% of respondents had "personally experienced or knew of colleagues who had a rogue trustee on their board" (Moltz, 2009).

The behaviors of rogues can vary (depending on who's describing them), from relatively benign (meddlesome, micromanaging) to malicious (attacking or undermining the president and/or the board). And although they can be elected or appointed, elected rogues are especially problematic because they typically can only be removed by the electorate or when their terms end. Therefore, they can do a lot of damage over both the short and long term.

Start With Basic Selection Criteria

It is common practice for institutions with self-perpetuating boards to build a roster of talented individuals. Distinguished alumni, community members, and corporate and nonprofit leaders are cultivated for future board openings. Institutions typically match potential board members against a list of criteria that includes demographic characteristics (e.g., age, gender, race/ethnicity); geographic location (e.g., nearby, state, region, international); and field of expertise (e.g., financial, real estate, social media, information technology, public relations, health care, and even higher education).

Some colleges and universities add other criteria to the mix:

- Resource development capacity (e.g., ability to get/connections to resources, ability to give)
- Oversight expertise (e.g., risk management, compliance, legal, investment/audit)
- Knowledge of key audiences (e.g., current or former charity CEO; former college president; corporate partner; foundation/grant-maker; large community-based nonprofit)

Boards with a range of expertise and characteristics tend to govern better than those that are quite homogenous.

For public universities, which must accept political appointees, it is good practice for presidents and board chairs to identify areas of strength and weakness in their board's composition and meet with the governor's appointment staff to discuss what to consider in making appointments. Some public institutions go a step further and develop a list of individuals who meet stated criteria and take those names to the governor.

Add Competencies

Savvy boards and presidents are moving beyond individual demographics and field of expertise (and individual wealth) to get to actual individual governance competencies—in other words, the ability to do the job. A report from the American Hospital Association (2009) provides an excellent distillation of some key competencies that should be sought in all hospital board members and that apply equally well to higher education trustees. They include accountability, collaboration, innovative thinking, complexity management, organizational awareness, professionalism, relationship-building, strategic orientation, information-seeking, change leadership, and team leadership. For each of these competencies, the report defines the individual trustee competency, lists behaviors associated with the competency, and provides sample interview questions to identify the competency in a prospective trustee. Let's take *innovative thinking* as an example.

> *Defined*: The ability to apply complex concepts, develop creative solutions, or adapt previous solutions in new ways for breakthroughs in the field.
>
> *Behaviors*: Makes complex ideas or situations clear, simple, or understandable, as in reframing a problem or using an analogy; fosters creation of new concepts that may not be obvious to others to explain situations or resolve problems; looks at things in new ways that yield new or innovative approaches—breakthrough thinking; shifts the paradigm; starts a new line of thinking; encourages these behaviors in others.
>
> *Sample interview questions*: Think of a situation or situations where you were involved in reinventing or creating a new program, product, or service.
>
> - How did you identify and help others understand all of the factors contributing to the need to reinvent the existing resource or to create something completely new?
> - How did you help make complex ideas or situations more clear or understandable?
> - How did you help explain problems or obstacles in ways that may not have been obvious to others?

- How did you help others involved in the creative process look at things in new ways?
- Have you participated in a process of breakthrough thinking and what role did you play in the process?

The American Hospital Association report also provides an example from Presbyterian Healthcare Services (PHS) of the competency-based governance model in use with sitting members where trustees are evaluated against expected individual competencies. Some of the items listed as PHS's board member competencies and description (American Hospital Association, 2009) are shown in Table 4.2.

Another example comes from the YMCA, which has developed a Board Leadership Competency Model (YMCA, 2009/2010). The model includes four overarching areas of importance: mission advancement, collaboration, operational effectiveness, and personal growth. Underneath each of those is a set of competencies including definitions and checklists.

For example, a competency under collaboration is *inclusion*, defined as embracing contributions from a wide range of people; its checklist includes the following items (among others):

- Embraces the differences of all people (i.e., culture, ability, ethnicity, religion, sexual orientation, gender, age, nation of origin, etc.)
- Treats all people with dignity and respect
- Builds consensus by intentionally listening and engaging in diverse perspectives

TABLE 4.2
PHS Board Member Competencies and Descriptions

Competency	Description
Team player	Encourages and facilitates cooperation within the board
Demonstrated commitment to the mission, vision, values, and ethical responsibilities to the community served by PHS	Uses Presbyterian's Vision, Values, Purpose, Strategies and the PHS Plan as a basis for discussions and decisions
Demonstrated willingness to devote the time necessary for board work, including board education	Welcomes requests for work to be completed at other times than board meetings

Source: American Hospital Association. (2009), p. 39.

- Promotes cooperation and collaboration with other organizations to achieve mutual benefits to all stakeholders
- Advocates for and designs the strategic vision that reflects the diverse needs and concerns of the whole community

Put Competencies Into Action

Some colleges and universities are already moving in the direction of individual board member competencies. For example, Robert Morris University (Pittsburgh, Pennsylvania) has added a list of "demonstrated inclusion competencies" to its board composition matrix that also includes more traditional characteristics such as alumni status, professional background, and demographics (internal documents, not for publication). And, in fact, most higher education boards would be well served by adding an individual competency approach to their current trustee recruitment and screening efforts.

For instance, the governance or trusteeship committee could begin by determining and defining the competencies that are most needed for effective board dialogues and decisions and then seek feedback from the rest of the board members, key administrators, and faculty leaders who interact regularly with the board.

The next step would be to identify the corresponding behaviors that demonstrate each competency or skill. The board could then use its list to assess both current board members and future board members against the competencies with an eye to where there are gaps (for prospective trustees to fill). The list could also identify areas for current trustee education or training and develop a plan to build trustee competence. Ideally, seek trustees "who are productively neurotic, . . . who are *self*-motivated and *self*-disciplined, . . . who wake up every day, compulsively driven to do the best they can because it is simply part of their DNA" (Collins, 2005, p. 15).

Conclusion

Boards are groups, and the best boards function like teams. The best teams understand the contributions of each team member and have expectations for the skills and competencies each must bring. Similarly, the best boards pay close attention to what each individual brings to the table—not only in terms of background, skill sets, demographic characteristics, and functional areas of expertise but also the competencies that encompass that person's ability to function as part of a high-performing board.

Questions for Boards

1. What individual competencies are most important for service on your board?
2. How can you best screen for those competencies?
3. To what extent does your orientation prepare individuals for all of the work of trusteeship? How can you ensure trustees have the necessary foundational knowledge to be effective in the role?

For Further Insight

To follow up on some of the issues raised in this chapter, we suggest:

- Chapter 1: The Evolving Board: Ways to Think About Governing Today
- Chapter 3: Is Your Board Mediocre?
- Chapter 5: Right Answers; Wrong Questions
- Chapter 8: Curiosity: The Boardroom's Missing Element
- Chapter 10: The Culture of Boards: Making the Invisible Visible

RIGHT ANSWERS;
WRONG QUESTIONS

Trustees and presidents expect a lot from governance, yet many know that their boards are underperforming—that the board could and should do more. Yet many of the questions we hear from presidents and board leaders seem to be the *wrong* ones such as: What is the right number of board members? How often should the board meet? Do we have the right committees and the right number of committees? These questions, although somewhat off-target, are well intended. After addressing those questions (and what lies beneath them), we propose (and answer) an alternative set of questions we think boards *should* discuss.

Commonly Asked "Wrong" Questions

It's true that governing well is a complicated undertaking that requires intentionality and commitment and that asking thoughtful, informed questions is important to continued improvement. Many of our conversations with presidents and board leaders in the United States and abroad who wish to improve governance typically include a set of questions about which institutional leaders seek answers. Although we applaud the interest and the endeavor, it strikes us that many of the most commonly asked questions may actually be the *wrong* ones to pursue, primarily because the answers won't actually help improve governance.

How Large Should the Board Be?

As discussed in chapter 1, this question typically comes up early in the conversations, particularly from presidents or board leaders at independent institutions with large boards. It seems that board size captures the attention of many trustees looking to improve how their boards govern. Our answer to the question about board size is, "Just big enough." (That response reminds us of a faculty member in our doctoral program who, when asked how long papers should be, said, "Just long enough"—much to the frustration of the students in the class.) A board should be large enough to address the work the institution faces, but not so large that governance becomes unwieldy, just like the size of a well-written essay. Cover the ground you need to cover and then wrap it up. Determining board size is as much an experiment as it is anything else. Boards interested in changing their size might consider the following:

- The ideal size is one that ensures a variety of perspectives on an increasingly large number of complex topics. Boards operate best when there are a variety of perspectives that can be called into service depending on the issues on the table (Russell Reynolds Associates, 2009). Boards with individuals who all think the same way, come from similar backgrounds, or have comparable professional experiences are at risk for potentially harmful blind spots. Boards able to develop and benefit from diverse ways of thinking and a range of knowledge and skill sets are better prepared to address the unknown.
- Boards need enough trustees to do the many tasks of governing but not so many that people do not see a role for themselves. Governance can be time-consuming and requires the hands, as well as the heads, of numerous people. At the same time, boards that do not find ways to engage all trustees risk disenfranchisement.
- The board needs to be of the right size to develop a positive culture and camaraderie among board members. How boards interact (as we explore in different chapters throughout this book) is essential to effective governance. Board size can either play a positive role in board member interaction or a negative one.
- Board size needs to be such that it allows the board to work effectively and efficiently. Effectiveness and efficiency are two different concepts and both size and structure contribute to both. Boards need to be efficient in that they often have a tremendous amount of work to accomplish in a relatively short period, given how most boards structure committee and board meetings. But as we note elsewhere, boards also need to be effective. They require sufficient numbers to establish a quorum, populate committees, periodically review the work of the board, and get their work done.

However, we believe that the number of individuals sitting on a board is less relevant to its effectiveness than other factors addressed later in the chapter.

How Often Should the Board Meet?

The frequency with which a board meets is a second question, also well intended, but not particularly useful. Our answer parallels the previous one: "Just frequently enough" to get the needed work done. As Chait (2009) said, "Some boards, eager to be more effective, decide to meet more often, while other boards for the very same reason decide to meet less frequently" (p. 10). Rather than focus on a fixed number of meetings, boards should consider the work they need to accomplish over the next 12 to 18 months and then determine the best way to structure board engagement to ensure that issues, whether planned for or yet to emerge, can be addressed sufficiently. We recognize that board and committee meetings require staff time, the focused attention of busy leaders, and the time commitment of trustees, but too many meetings result in "make-work" or a lot of very long, detailed (and sometimes boring) presentations by senior staff or show-and-tell sessions involving students and faculty. Overly frequent meetings may also open the door for micromanaging as the board may be looking for work and take focus beyond governance into management or operations.

Too few meetings can also create challenges. Board agendas become overly full, there is little time for discussion and engagement on complex issues, and board members become too distanced from the institution and the factors that should shape those discussions. Furthermore, the foundation of trustee collaboration and trust may need to be reestablished if the time between meetings is too long. This becomes particularly problematic if trustees often miss meetings due to schedule conflicts. Having too few meetings may be a recipe for disengagement.

Finally, given the excellent virtual meeting technology that exists, not all board or committee meetings need to be face-to-face.

Do We Have the Right Committees and the Right Number of Committees?

Many presidents and board leaders worry about their committee structure, and they often ask these questions in comparison to other boards. Some presidents wonder if they have too many committees. The largest we'd heard of was 18 committees on a board of 25 or so trustees governing a residential undergraduate college. Each trustee on that board was expected to serve on at least 3 committees. Trustees went to a lot of meetings; and sometimes, given the excessive demands on trustee time, committees had only 1 or 2 trustees present. Thus, their committees struggled to function well.

Other presidents and board members wonder if they need to increase the number of committees. Do we need a technology committee? A risk committee? An enrollment committee? What about civic engagement? Do academic affairs and student affairs need to be combined or should they be separate? Our answer: Committees matter only in light of the work boards are doing. What are the strategic and fiduciary issues the board needs to address? Where will those issues be given the attention they require? How can you ensure key issues do not fall through the gaps between committees or that multiple committees aren't discussing the same issues, creating redundancy or, worse, different pathways forward?

Furthermore, comparing board structure is difficult, as there are many factors that shape boards and board committees. Some boards at very similar institutions look very different in size and committee structure. And some very different institutions have similarly structured boards. The extent to which boards add value may only partially depend on structure. A complex university with a larger board may function at a higher level than a similarly complex university with a very small board, simply because a small board doesn't have the time and capacity to address issues as fully as a larger, more comprehensively structured board. Time on task matters. That said, given all of the factors that shape board effectiveness that we explore throughout this book, committee structure might actually contribute little.

Should Faculty or Students Serve on the Board?

A final question frequently asked relates to faculty and student membership on boards. Having either, or both, is more the exception than the rule. We believe it is important to ensure that many perspectives are voiced in the boardroom. Boards make better decisions with more complete information and sometimes that information is best provided directly by students and faculty. However, voice does not equate with vote. And currently employed individuals, as well as students (or even parents of currently enrolled students for that matter), can too easily adopt a stakeholder mind-set rather than a fiduciary one. Stakeholders are often too concerned about the present or the parties they believe they are representing. Furthermore, such seats on boards tend to be only a single seat. This means there is a single perspective from the group, which may or may not be accurate or represent the views of the faculty or the students.

There are ways to ensure voice and a larger number of voices. For example, having faculty leaders serve on select board committees is one strategy. One board with which we worked has a faculty representative sitting on the academic affairs committee, a different faculty representative serving on the student affairs committee, and a third working on the finance committee. The board also had a pattern of inviting faculty to focused discussions on key topics for which they thought faculty perspective would be essential.

Holding focused meetings, and even open forums with faculty and with students, is a second strategy. Finally, creating ad hoc or board-level task forces that include membership of key campus individuals is a third strategy.

What These Questions Are Really Asking

These questions are well intended even if they are not necessarily helpful. But what's behind the questions is enlightening, so we recast them as follows:

- How can boards develop robust formats to most effectively govern?
- Through what approaches can boards ensure that the limited time available is well spent on meaningful issues that demand attention?
- How can boards ensure the right voices, perspectives, and expertise exist on the board, and that all members are effectively engaged?
- How should boards organize themselves to accomplish meaningful governance?

How one frames the questions is essential to finding good answers. As iconic designer at General Motors, Charles Kettering, is noted for saying, "A problem well-stated is a problem half-solved."

We offer ways to think about these questions at different points throughout this book. For example, chapter 6 on board agendas offers suggestions on spending board meeting time effectively. Chapter 4 on competencies and chapter 10 on board culture address issues of ensuring voice and multiple perspectives.

The Right Questions to Ask

Given that we framed this chapter as "wrong" questions, we're often asked, "What are the "right" ones?" Although there are many questions that might be asked about governance, there are four we believe boards should prioritize.

How Well Is the Board Performing?

Great boards have the capacity to look in the collective mirror, understand with intentionality how well they are working, and think critically about the value their efforts are bringing to the university, college, or state system. Boards should put in place robust assessment processes, collect data about group and individual board member performance, and use the findings to continuously improve. This should be the responsibility of the governance committee. Good practice says that trustee leaders take responsibility for board performance, regularize performance conversations and assessments, ensure that the board receives feedback, develop strategies to improve, and then act on those strategies.

To Whom Is the Board Accountable and How Can It Demonstrate Its Accountability?

A criticism of too many boards is the lack of accountability for their efforts. The board holds the ultimate legal and fiduciary responsibility for the institutions they hold in the public trust. Boards hold presidents accountable for performance, but board accountability is less defined. Therefore, essential to their work is ensuring the public trust. Being transparent in their deliberations, using data well, engaging stakeholders, and having high ethical standards are important to this greater sense of board accountability. Once a board loses trust with key stakeholders, it is difficult and time-consuming to recapture.

It is essential to note that accountability is ultimately a legal threshold, but boards are responsible for ensuring that the views of stakeholders are heard and considered, and that the board and administration act in the best interests of the institution. (We explore the issue of accountability in more depth in chapter 7.)

To What Extent Is the Board Spending Its Time on the Right Issues?

Given the numbers and complexity of issues facing higher education today and into the foreseeable future, boards are faced with too many challenges rather than too few. Neither underengagement nor underperformance is acceptable. Understanding the strategic priorities of the university and the fiduciary responsibilities of governance, and focusing board work on, those matters, is essential. It is important to realize that the board's preference regarding how much time to spend on a given issue will likely change over time. What is important next year may be less important in five years, and boards with the ability to adapt, respond, and pivot will outperform those mired in nostalgic conversations about yesterday's topics.

Relevant boards will need the structures and capacities to allow for flexibility and adaptation; this may mean fewer standing committees and more ad hoc task forces, or a committee structure that can flex to align with the priorities of the institution or system. For example, a board might align its work around key issues such as financial sustainability; compliance, risk, and accountability; the student experience; academic excellence; economic impact and relevance; and other issues specific to the university, such as academic health centers or mission. The bottom line is that it doesn't matter how the board is organized or who sits on it if the board doesn't know what it should be doing or where its primary focus should be.

To What Extent Does the Board Have the Right Culture?

Too often boards that are seeking improvement focus on changing structures—either the organizational structure or the meeting structure. However, what might be more meaningful to alter, and surely more challenging, is the culture of the board. Culture is that often invisible set of behaviors and beliefs that shapes board dynamics, such as who speaks, about what issues, and with what effect, and is taught to new generations of trustees, sometimes intentionally, but other times not. A positive culture that promotes inclusivity of people and ideas, reflection and discussion, constructive disagreement, and strong sense of purpose can help boards leap ahead. At the same time, a dysfunctional culture of backroom decision-making, poor engagement, fervent convictions and personal agendas, and incivility between board members or between the board and the administration can set governance back light-years. When a disruptive culture impedes governance by asking questions such as whether the board should meet three or four times a year or if the academic and student affairs committees should be merged or separate, its practices become insufficient or even a distraction. Poor culture is poor culture and it prevents effective governance, period (for more about board culture, see chapter 10).

Conclusion: Keep Asking Questions of All Types

One of the essential traits of highly successful boards is that they learn how to ask meaningful and focused questions, a skill that can be difficult to master. But it is those boards and presidents who stop asking questions—or only ask a narrow slice of questions—that most worry us. Boards can and should develop the capacity to ask a range of good questions and to recognize when those questions add value rather than move the board in an unconstructive direction. Trustees should practice the art of asking questions rather than simply asserting opinions. Great questions lead to meaningful conversations, which in turn result in better governance (for more, see chapter 8 on board curiosity).

Questions for Boards

1. How does the board determine the most important issues on which to spend its time?

2. To what extent is the board spending its time on the most important issues?
3. How can the board ensure an appropriate balance of fiduciary oversight and strategic foresight?
4. To what extent does the board have a culture of accountability?

For Further Insight

To follow up on some of the issues raised in this chapter, we suggest:

- Chapter 1: The Evolving Board: Ways to Think About Governing Today
- Chapter 6: Spending Scarce Time Wisely
- Chapter 7: Ensuring Accountability for the Board by the Board
- Chapter 8: Curiosity: The Boardroom's Missing Element
- Chapter 10: The Culture of Boards: Making the Invisible Visible
- Chapter 14: Strategy, Higher Education, and Boards (and Forget Planning)

6

SPENDING SCARCE
TIME WISELY

I t's no surprise that what happens in board meetings is essential to the impact boards have on the institutions they serve. Time is one of the most precious commodities trustees have and one that, if squandered, can result in trustee disengagement and organizational mediocrity. Ideally, board meetings are events that trustees look forward to as opportunities to add critical insight on the most important issues facing the institution. The president and staff, in turn, look forward to meetings to enrich their thinking and move the institution or state system ahead. These notions place a premium on the meeting agenda as the tool to ensure efficiency and effectiveness. This chapter provides ideas to help institutions get the most from meetings by being intentional about outcomes and structuring activities to achieve stated goals.

Making Smart Choices

A common refrain from college and university trustees is that while they love serving and visiting campus for board meetings three or four times a year for private colleges and universities and eight or nine times annually for public boards, it is less for the meetings themselves and more to spend time with colleagues and friends. For alumni trustees—almost 50% at public and private universities (Association of Governing Boards of Universities and Colleges, 2016)—returning to campus brings back those "good old" college days. When it comes to board meetings, though, trustees often admit that they are boring and worse. Common refrains include the following:

> We spend most of our time viewing lengthy PowerPoints and listening to committee reports.

Board meetings are a regurgitation of the president and [vice president] reports.

Our meeting time is spent, sadly, in the weeds. I'm not sure that we really want to dive into operations, but that's where we typically end up and it's frustrating for everyone (trustees and senior staff alike).

Our meetings, while always informative, tend to ramble off topic and often into the details. Sometimes it's because trustees' questions lead into operations and other times it seems that important information is not in the reports we're hearing, so we press for more.

I feel like, too often, we lose track of why we're there and on what we're supposed to focus.

I wonder if we don't spend too much time in weeds at the committee level and not enough in-depth on important matters at the full board level.

Our board meetings are rehashes of committee meetings that, in the spirit of openness, transparency, and inclusion are open to everyone, and all trustees attend! So, we have the same conversations twice.

One university trustee was particularly graphic:

Quarterly meetings are long. . . . It's like the Bataan Death March; we go all day and all night.

And although trustees are bored and frustrated, presidents and cabinet members have their own issues with meetings, as indicated in the following comments:

We sometimes wonder if trustees have an idea how much work goes into board meetings—before with preparation, during the meetings guiding them through material, and after with follow-up activities. When you add in committee meetings with staff liaisons (a nice word for "do all the work"), vice presidents spend a lot of their working lives dealing with matters that are peripheral to the student and faculty experience. Don't get me wrong; we are all grateful for our trustees who are, after all, volunteers (and donors to boot), but leadership spends an inordinate amount of time planning and delivering board and committee meetings without seeing much fruit from the labor.

As campus CFO, I prepare a lot of financial performance data to share with trustees at board meetings. I try to make sure that it's digestible for those less savvy about the numbers but sophisticated enough for the investment bankers in the room—a tough balance for sure. But, honestly, most of the time it seems everyone's eyes sort of glaze over.

We have a board portal that allows us to see which trustees have logged on to read postings before meetings and how long they spend on it. I was astonished to learn that the majority of our trustees were not even reading the President's Report and I called them on it. As president, I'm not saying that my word is the gospel, but I did have to question, "If they're not reading that, are they reading anything?"

Key themes emerged across these all-too-common examples: (a) too much reporting and not enough meaningful dialogue, (b) too much focus on operations ("the weeds"), (c) lack of focus and meandering discussions, and (d) trustees not being uniformly prepared. These are all the death knell for board meetings. But each can be addressed with forethought and attention.

Trustee Engagement

An important goal of effective board and committee meetings is more meaningful trustee engagement on mission-relevant topics, the purpose of which is for trustees to add value that leads to better decisions and institutional outcomes. The goal is not just more engagement for engagement sake. After all, well-intentioned but ill-informed trustees engaging on peripheral topics does not advance good governance or produce progress on institutional aims. It simply keeps trustees busy and in worst-case scenarios leads to problems in the boardroom. Distracted boards can be disruptive boards. What steps can boards take to ensure better meetings? In an article for AGB's *Trusteeship* magazine, Trower (2015) offered 10 steps to ensure better trustee engagement at meetings. Two are especially relevant with respect to agendas.

Make Board Meeting Goals Explicit

The first step is to make meeting goals explicit, and it's amazing how powerful this can be in ensuring more productive board meetings. Simon Sinek (2009) noted, "Start with why." Stephen Covey (1989) elaborated: "Begin with the end in mind" (p. 97). It's advantageous to be explicit about intentions and then communicate them. When setting a board meeting agenda, begin with these questions: Why are we having this board meeting? What does the president need from the board? What does the board need from the president? What do we want to accomplish as a group?

Making goals explicit will assist with all four of the key themes stated previously. It's important to communicate meeting objectives to the board on the agenda and at the beginning of the meeting. The outcomes might be clear and transparent in the minds of those creating the agenda, but too often boards create habits and then become trapped in them. Many trustees tell us their board agendas always follow the same general outline, which greatly limits the crucial element of curiosity (see chapter 8 for a deeper discussion). Being clear on why you are discussing each item and what the intended direction might be (without making the decision prior to the discussion) is important. Some boards identify agenda items as one of three types: (a) for your information, (b) brainstorming or problem-solving, and (c) deciding/ action items. For example, a board discussion about enrollment trends might be to (a) inform the board of demographic trends that trustees should know about, (b) engage the board in thinking about new strategies to expand the reach of the admissions office, or (c) determine the policy for merit-based aid. One topic, three types of conversations, each different. The more explicit board leaders and presidents can be about why they are spending board time on each issue, the better. Simple notations on board agendas can be very helpful tools for signaling the forthcoming use of time.

Design the Meeting Agenda to Meet the Goals

The second step is to design the agenda around the key issues and stated goals. Doing so keeps the board focused on what it's there to do and minimizes drift into management details or sidetracking into personal agendas or pet issues of individual trustees. See the examples from Wheaton College (Norton, Massachusetts) in Figures 6.1 and 6.2 and from Carlow University (Pittsburgh, Pennsylvania) in Figure 6.3 for examples of intentionally constructed board meetings. (Full disclosure: Trower served on the Board of Trustees of Wheaton from 2012 to 2017 and has also served as a consultant to Carlow University.)

In addition to stated goals, the Wheaton agendas are noteworthy for (a) using plenary sessions of the board for key conversations; (b) including a student performance (in February); (c) engaging the board in meaningful conversations with faculty through "table talks" about faculty publications, classes, special projects, innovations in pedagogy and student engagement, cutting-edge research, and so on; and (d) providing important social time for just board and president and for board and senior staff. For plenary session topics, the trustees completed homework including advance readings and familiarizing themselves with data. They were given questions to consider while reading and reviewing the data. This approach allowed the board to "hit the ground running" during these sessions and to set expectations for the forthcoming discussions. To further facilitate the board work, the board used breakout sessions for smaller group work, which was especially important to get all trustees engaged in the issues and with each other.

Figure 6.1. Wheaton College (Massachusetts) board of trustees meeting agenda, February 2017.

In addition to the many regular board matters, the board will focus on several items that relate very specifically to our strategic plan and to our long-term goals. The objectives arising out of these discussions include:

1. Seek trustee support for a multiyear facilities investment plan. The plan will identify and prioritize the key campus needs, goals, and objectives over a 5- and 10-year period.
2. Review the status of the ongoing branding process and take a vote to endorse the overall direction, approach, and strategy.
3. Build trustee consensus on a multiyear approach to fostering a greater culture of philanthropy and growing our fund-raising capacity to levels that can be sustained over time.
4. Analyze and evaluate faculty, staff, and student recruitment and retention data to guide current and future discussions related to building a diverse and inclusive campus.
5. Create a long-term vision to guide building the board of the future. This will include prioritizing desired qualities in future board members and determining how to identify, foster, and develop potential members with these qualities.
6. Engage directly with the faculty to learn more about the variety of ways that their scholarship and professional activities shape Wheaton College and the world.

Thursday, February 9, 2017
5:00–6:00 p.m. Governance Committee (members)
6:00–8:00 p.m. Dinner at the President's House

Friday, February 10, 2017
7:00   a.m. Breakfast
7:25– 8:25 a.m. Audit Committee (members)
8:30–10:00 a.m. Finance & Facilities Committee (open) [Goal 1]
10:15–11:30 a.m. Educational Quality & Student Experience Committee (open) [Goal 4]
11:30–12:30 p.m. Lunch
12:30– 1:45 p.m. Reach & Reputation Committee (open) [Goals 2 and 3]
2:00– 3:30 p.m. Plenary Session: Board of the Future [Goal 5]
3:30– 5:00 p.m. Faculty Session: Vote on Tenure and Table Talks [Goal 6]

5:00–6:00	p.m.	Reception With Faculty and President's Council
6:00–8:00	p.m.	Student Performance and Dinner

Saturday, February 11, 2017
7:00	a.m.	Breakfast
7:15–8:25	a.m.	Philanthropy Committee (members)
8:30–12:00	p.m.	Meeting of the Board of Trustees

The Carlow University board undertook a similar strategy. It identified a set of objectives and connected each of those items with time on the agenda. In addition, the trustees were informed ahead of the meeting about what they would be discussing (e.g., the revised Mission, Values, and Philosophy Statement and the new Academic Undergraduate Core Curriculum) so that trustees were prepared and focused. Further, this agenda clearly separated time for discussion (this meeting) from time for decision (next meeting). The agenda allowed time for the board to assess the meeting and for an executive session with the president. (See Figure 6.3.)

In addition to what is noted in the prior paragraph, the Carlow agenda is noteworthy for (a) including a "Mission Moment" (an example of how the institution is making an impact; this might include a student performance, a student talking about her experience, or a faculty member discussing a new pedagogy), (b) clearly stating agenda items where action is required (e.g., where a vote is needed), (c) utilizing a "Consent Agenda" for routine items that do not require board discussion (e.g., minutes from the prior meeting and committee reports), (d) quick reports from committees (for items of which the board should be aware), (e) noting important dates and board meeting schedule, (f) allowing more time for items requiring discussion (items VI, VII, and XII in Figure 6.3), and (g) posing questions for discussion for the two most important items (the new Mission, Values, and Philosophy Statement and the new Academic Undergraduate Core Curriculum). Teeing up discussion questions for trustees to consider in advance of the meeting is an especially effective springboard to dialogue and is far better than asking, "Are there any questions?" at the end of a presentation (a strategy which tends to generate very little discussion except for a few clarifying questions or blank stares).

Another strategy that helps boards stay focused and manage attention is to adopt the six-box format for board work (see Figure 6.4). A strategy coach in the *McKinsey Quarterly* argued that senior leaders have limited attention and they must use this resource carefully (Bregman, 2013). He argued that "the most destructive myth in time management is that you can get everything

Figure 6.2. Wheaton College (Massachusetts) board of trustees meeting agenda, May 2017.

Meeting Goals and Agenda

1. Review and endorse a plan to guide investments in faculty and staff over the next five years, designed to meet our strategic objective of recruiting, developing, and retaining a world-class faculty and staff.
2. Discuss the planning and process for moving forward with the first 3 facilities projects in our 10-year facilities investment plan (residence hall, campus center, admission building) and approve the funding and parameters of the design phase for each.
3. Receive the report of the Inclusion and Diversity Task Force, using it to set and endorse priorities for immediate next steps by linking it to the various diversity objectives in our strategic plan.
4. In anticipation of a deeper discussion at the July retreat, begin the discussion on the major fund-raising priorities for the next three years and approve the next steps for a preliminary analysis that will help inform the work at the retreat.
5. Review the progress and time line on curriculum revision and the work being done to more fully integrate the curricular and cocurricular experience of our students.
6. Seek board approval on new trustees and board leadership, and engage the entire board in a discussion on term and age limits and the role of trustees in various decision-making processes.

Thursday, May 18, 2017
5:00–6:00   p.m. Governance Committee (members)
6:00–8:00   p.m. Dinner at the President's House

Friday, May 19, 2017
7:00   a.m. Breakfast
7:25– 8:25 a.m. Audit Committee (members)
8:30– 9:20 a.m. Educational Quality & Student Experience Committee (open) [Goal 3]
9:30–10:20 a.m. Finance & Facilities Committee (open) [Goal 2]
10:30–11:20 a.m. Plenary Session: Human Capital [Goal 1]
11:30–12:20 p.m. Reach & Reputation Committee (open) [Goal 4]
12:30– 3:00 p.m. Meeting of the Board of Trustees (working lunch) [Goals 5 and 6]
3:30– 5:00 p.m. Posse Graduation

5:00–6:00	p.m. President's Reception for the Class of 2017 & Families
6:00–7:00	p.m. Leadership Reception With the President
7:15–9:30	p.m. Dinner
	Trustees, Spouses, Honorary Degree Recipients, Guests, and President's Council

Saturday, May 20, 2017
 Commencement

done" (p. 2). He advised that leaders use 6 boxes to organize their work by noting the top 5 priorities, 1 in each box, and spending 95% of the board's time on those items. The remaining work can go into a sixth box labeled "Other 5%." Why? "Because getting things done is all about focus" (p. 2). Boards too can benefit by focusing, particularly if the institution is facing a number of serious issues and choices. Without focus of the type described here, boards drift from issue to issue and do not give the essential items sufficient time.

This tool was helpful for a board that decided its meeting agendas were too driven by crisis. Constantly reacting to the latest crisis (the urgent), they couldn't find the discipline to focus on what was important. A board-wide conversation with the president and the senior team yielded 5 priorities for the board over an 18-month period. And the "six-box" approach provided them with the structure they needed to be disciplined about what to put on their agendas. Although boards do need to do more than 5 tasks and they must respond to emerging issues (particularly crises), the exercise of forced choices helped them think differently about how to design meeting agendas and distribute their time. This activity also helped them delegate work to committees and in turn helped some committees restructure their work.

Solutions Seeking Problems

The trustees and staff members quoted at the start of this chapter highlighted common problems associated with board meetings. The examples noted address meetings that drift and those that devolve into operations. Having clear outcomes and developing the meeting intentionally to address those outcomes help to resolve those familiar concerns.

Two additional common problems remain: meetings at which trustees are unprepared for the work at hand and meetings that spend too much time on presentations (trustees being talked at instead of talked with). The following strategies can help address those problems.

Figure 6.3. Carlow University (Pennsylvania) Board of Trustees meeting agenda, January 2015.

AGENDA, Monday, January 26, 2015, 4:00 p.m.–7:00 p.m.

Goals:

1. Discuss and provide feedback to the proposed new Academic Undergraduate Core Curriculum/General Education with vote by board at next board meeting (substantive change in academic program).
2. Discuss and approve new philosophy statement, revised mission, and values.
3. Monitor current implementation of new strategic plan.
4. Review current financial status of university at end of second quarter.
5. Approve proposed tuition and fees rates for FY16.

   I. Call to Order and Welcome (15 minutes)
- Reflection
- Mission Moment

  II. Consent Agenda (3 minutes)
- Approval of October 13, 2014 Minutes (action required)

III. President's Report (20 minutes)
- Executive Summary Highlights—Update on Strategic Plan implementation

IV. March 21, 2015, Board Governance Retreat Desired Outcomes (5 minutes)

  V. Financial Status of University (15 minutes)
- Current financial status (action required)
- Status of University Commons Building project

VI. Mission, Values, and New Philosophy Statement (action required) (30 minutes)
- How do the revised mission, values, and new philosophy statement align with the university's purpose and the vision for the university moving forward?
- What ideas do you have for how we apply the revised mission, values, and philosophy?

VII. Presentation and Discussion of New Core Curriculum (30 minutes)
- How will this new core curriculum align with the strategic plan, academic quality, and high-impact practices in higher education?

- How does the board see this new core curriculum contributing to differentiating us as a university and serving the public good?
- What insights and feedback does the board have for the proposed curriculum?
- What other issues need to be considered prior to approval and implementation?

VIII. Update on Middle States Self-Study and Expectations of the Board (10 minutes)

IX. Board Committee Reports (Committee Chairs) (15 minutes)
- Set tuition rate for 2015–2016 (action required)
- Corporate resolution—change in signatories (action required)
- Approval of trustee term extension (action required)
- Report from Development & Cultivation Committee
- Other committee recommendations for future board action or deliberation

X. Board Evaluation of Meeting (7 minutes)

XI. Adjournment

XII. Executive Session (Trustees only) (30 minutes)

DATES TO REMEMBER:

Alumni Scholarship Lunch—Saturday, February 28, 2015—11:30 a.m., Pittsburgh Athletic Association.

All-Day Board Retreat: Saturday, March 21, 2015, 8:15–5:15 p.m. BNY Mellon Bank (downtown Pittsburgh) with external facilitator.

Scholarship Day and Honors Convocation—Tuesday, April 21, 2015: Scholarship presentations: 10:00 a.m.–3:00 p.m.; Honors Convocation: 3:30 p.m.; Graduate Colloquium: 5:30 p.m.

Carlow Laureates Lunch: Friday, May 8, 2015, noon. Location to be determined.

Spring Commencement: Saturday, May 9, 2015: Baccalaureate Mass: 10:00 a.m., St. Paul Cathedral; Commencement: 1:00 p.m., Soldiers and Sailors Memorial Hall.

BOARD MEETING SCHEDULE FOR 2014–15:

Saturday, March 21, 2015: All-day facilitated Board Retreat (8:15 a.m.–5:15 p.m. BNY Mellon (Trustees only).

Monday, June 15, 2015, 4:00 p.m., Arcade Room.

Figure 6.4. A "six-box" approach for board meeting priorities.

Priority 1	Priority 2	Priority 3
Priority 4	Priority 5	Other 5%

Trustees Are Unprepared

One newly hired university executive vice president (EVP) complained about poorly constructed board meetings. Before each discussion item, the president would ask the board members to review pages 5 through 20, or pages 57 through 83, for example. The EVP thought this a tremendous waste of valuable meeting time (and we do, too). Yet the president insisted that this was the best way to get trustees to read the materials. There are other ways to ensure that trustees are well prepared and ready to engage. Helpful strategies include the following:

1. Make preparedness an explicit expectation for trustees and hold them accountable. Being clear in the recruitment process and in new trustee orientation that individuals are expected to have read the materials and come prepared to engage is an important step. As part of trustee evaluation (either conducted annually or at the middle and conclusion of their terms of service), provide feedback about the level of preparedness demonstrated at board meetings. Letting individuals know that preparedness is important and that it is being monitored sends strong messages to trustees.

2. Ensure that materials are sent with sufficient time for trustees to read them. Too often materials are sent at the last minute, leaving already busy people little time to read and digest them. (And, as noted in this chapter's introduction, monitoring via the board portal who opens materials when can be illustrative. But be aware of becoming the board's "Big Brother.")

3. Ensure an appropriate amount of materials. Too often board members don't read what is sent to them because the content is overly detailed and voluminous. Be selective about how much and what material you provide. (Then ask questions of board members to evaluate whether the

amount of material is just right, too much, or too little.) Another effective strategy is to consider two tiers of information: high-level executive summaries (to help trustees know where to focus their attention) and deeper supporting information (for those who want to read more and have the time to do so). This is also a helpful strategy for committee meetings as well as for committee members who might seek more information on a limited set of issues.

4. Frame board agendas around questions, as we mentioned previously. This enables trustees to "prepare for the test" by reading material with an eye to being able to participate in discussions around those key questions. (For more, see chapter 8 on curiosity in the boardroom.)

Too Many Presentations

Board meetings that consist of too many (or too long) presentations are rarely effective. The overreliance on presentations is a symptom of three common ailments:

1. Agendas are poorly constructed and don't have clear outcomes.
2. Administrators or board leaders don't really want board engagement and thus keep boards busy and distracted by presentations. (Trustees can do little damage when they are nodding off because of boredom.)
3. The board may not have the knowledge of higher education or the institution and its context to understand materials without thorough presentations by staff.

In each of these situations, board meeting agendas are filled with presentations, but the solutions are dependent on the ailment rather than the symptom. We've addressed the first one in terms of having clearly stated objectives (goals) for chapter meeting. The second ailment (where leaders do not really want trustee engagement) is a deeper-seated issue for which better agendas are not the solution. Rectifying this will require that board leadership speak candidly with the president to understand his or her point of view and clarify mutual expectations. (See chapter 12 for more information on the pivotal partnership between the president and the board.) With respect to the third, spend more time at orientation on what trustees need to know and offer information sessions (at board meetings or remotely between meetings) to help all board members gain stronger knowledge about the issues facing their institution or state system. (See our discussion in chapter 4 regarding new trustee orientation.)

The Final Ingredient: A Skilled Facilitator

One other factor resulting in less-than-productive meetings is that the skills of the individual chairing the meetings are lacking. We have all been in meetings where the chair lets discussions stray, doesn't curtail tangential (or sidebar) conversations, allows important lines of discussion to wither, and generally runs poor meetings. This sort of chairmanship is easy to spot and diagnose. In contrast, some meetings are noted for their efficiency and effectiveness; trustees are involved in substantive dialogue instead of watching the clock (or gazing out the window). At the end, those attending seem almost surprised that the meeting ended (and maybe even ended early). The best facilitators have a subtle yet forceful presence, are able to identify themes across discussions and artfully weave them together to lead to better insights, and skillfully stay on time without making people feel rushed or cut off.

Regardless of the magic that seems to surround well-facilitated, effective discussions, following are some steps that chairs can take to facilitate effective meetings:

1. Know the participants. Effective meeting chairs know the personalities, strengths, and weaknesses of those they are leading in discussion. They have a mental map of who will likely speak and on what, who will remain silent and needs to be invited into the conversation or encouraged to speak, and from whom the potential derailments might originate. Although it is not always possible to know everyone, it is helpful to have given the interpersonal dimensions of the group some thought before the meeting begins. Seasoned chairs do this.

2. Have a game plan, and a game plan for the game plan. Meeting chairs should use the agenda, as we've discussed, as the public and visible game plan for the meeting (with its logical order and stated objectives). But they are well served to also have a second plan for how they will execute the game plan that gets at how to approach and advance the needed conversations. What are the key issues that should be discussed, who might the chair call upon to move hard conversations forward or make progress on stalled decisions, and what is the desired pace of the discussion?

3. Work and think in two different points in time. Highly skilled discussion leaders are able to work and think in the present and in the future. They listen and attend to the immediate discussion (thinking in the present) and also think about where the discussion should be going and how to keep it on track (thinking in the future). They need to be able to

simultaneously keep these two points of time in their head as they move the discussion along.

4. Close effectively. The best meeting chairs are masters at drawing discussions to a close. Ending boardroom discussions has three key components, each of which should be done intentionally. Although the agenda and its objectives will frame the anticipated discussion, the concluding work of the chair is to summarize the discussion, secure a commitment to action, and recognize the very good contributions to the dialogue.

Conclusion

Boards have very little time to do their complex work, yet too many boards spend too much time in unproductive meetings. Too often, old meeting habits go unexamined and, therefore, unchecked. Board agendas follow well-trodden pathways with little deviation or questioning of why we meet this way and what we really seek to accomplish. Board work, as we write throughout this book, benefits greatly by intentionality. In few places is this truer than with respect to board meetings and board agendas. By breaking habitual patterns of how boards meet and what they discuss, boards may design better ways of governing and in turn find they are adding increasing value.

Questions for Boards

1. How effective are your meetings? How efficient are they? What evidence supports your answers?
2. How clear are your agendas and their intended outcomes? To what extent do you know what you are doing and why you are doing it?
3. What is the balance of time spent listening to reports, brainstorming, problem-finding and framing or problem-solving, and deciding on/taking action? Is this the right balance? How might you rebalance time on task?
4. How much board education occurs at board meetings? Does the board have sufficient information to do its work?
5. How might you frame possible questions for the board to consider *before* the meeting (as part of the agenda)?
6. Can the board identify and agree on its top five priorities and allocate time accordingly to focus appropriately on what matters most?
7. How frequently do meetings end with a summary from the board chair and president about what they heard and what's next?

For Further Insight

To follow up on some of the issues raised in this chapter, we suggest:

- Chapter 4: Individual Competencies for Collective Impact
- Chapter 8: Curiosity: The Boardroom's Missing Element
- Chapter 9: The "Jobs" of Committees: Of Drill Bits and Milkshakes
- Chapter 12: The Prime Partnership Between Presidents and Board Chairs
- Chapter 13: Creating the Capacity for Trying Issues
- Chapter 16: Governing Circa 1749

7

ENSURING ACCOUNTABILITY FOR THE BOARD BY THE BOARD

As we have showcased in prior chapters, the headlines show that no type of institution is exempt from governance woes and sometimes the intervention of attorneys general, governors, alumni, and more. At the heart of many of these situations is the challenge of board accountability. What is accountability when it comes to governance? To whom are boards accountable and for what? And how can they improve their accountability? The student learning movement has increased the emphasis on faculty accountability. Accreditation addresses institutional accountability. Board accountability has yet to garner the same attention. This chapter highlights how boards can get ahead of the accountability curve and, by so doing, greatly help their institutions.

What Is Meant by Board Accountability?

Most people involved in higher education are familiar with some form of accountability. The student learning movement has increased the emphasis on faculty accountability. Accreditation addresses institutional accountability. Although, in general, board accountability has yet to garner the same attention, it does occasionally. Accrediting agencies, for example, do call attention to board accountability, particularly when boards go off the rails. We believe that boards should be out ahead of the accountability curve. By doing so, they can increase their contributions to the institution by intercepting public criticism of the board or the institution, thereby mitigating fallout. Why wait for a crisis or outside intervention?

Here is the technical answer to the question of what is meant by board accountability: Because the institutions they govern are supported by public contributions and enjoy favorable tax treatment, higher education boards are legally bound by the duties of care (exercising diligent oversight, being prepared for meetings), loyalty (placing organizational interest over self-interest, ensuring no conflicts of interest), and obedience (staying true to the institution's mission, ensuring funds raised are used in support of the mission). The United Kingdom embeds governance "musts" into its governance code for all such bodies (see Box 7.1).

All academic institutions have articles of incorporation (bylaws) that describe the board as responsible for what the institution does and how it does it. Boards are answerable to federal, state, and local agencies and must file a Form 990 with the Internal Revenue Service that (a) provides an overview of institutional activities, programs, and governance and (b) discloses detailed financial information (Internal Revenue Service, 2017). Regional accreditation bodies also keep an eye on governance. Each institution's president serves at the pleasure of the board and is, therefore, accountable to the board for her or his performance but also that of the institution. Thus, the board is responsible for hiring, evaluating, supporting, compensating, and—when necessary—firing the president.

To Whom Is the Board Accountable?

First and foremost, because boards hold their institutions in the public trust, they are accountable to the public for achieving public purposes; this notion extends to independent and public colleges and universities. Boards that

BOX 7.1.
United Kingdom Governing Body Code of Governance

In the United Kingdom important beliefs are embedded in the Higher Education Code of Governance (Committee of University Chairs, 2014):

- The governing body will want to ensure the highest standards of ethical behaviour among its members, who **must** act ethically at all times in line with the accepted standards of behaviour in public life, and in the interests of the institution.
- Members of governing bodies **must** act, and be perceived to act, impartially, and not be influenced by social or business relationships.
- The governing body **must** ensure that its decision-making processes are free of any undue pressures from external groups, including donors, alumni, corporate sponsors and political interest groups (emphasis in original).

Source. Retrieved from https://www.universitychairs.ac.uk/wp-content/uploads/2015/02/Code-Final.pdf

end up in the headlines for misbehavior often do not violate legal statutes. Instead, they lose public trust. Board accountability has a public dimension to it beyond the technical aspects outlined previously. Boards need to behave in ways that ensure the public trusts them to act in the interest of the institution and that ensure they are doing their collective best to move the institution or state system forward. Although boards are often called upon to make difficult and controversial decisions, it often is the court of public opinion in which boards are judged.

At its most basic level, this public accountability is akin to government agencies answering to the electorate and businesses answering to stockholders. However, boards do not have electorates or stockholders who can readily demand greater accountability. Unlike stockholders or electorates, university stakeholders with a few exceptions lack direct levers of influence on boards. Although the faculty can vote no confidence in the board or board leadership, as was the case at the University of Wisconsin in 2016 (Savidge, 2016), they cannot vote out officials at the ballot box or use the tools of activist investors in the corporate setting. (The exception to this is at the handful of boards of four-year universities and colleges where trustees are actually elected, a more common process in community colleges.)

For What Is the Board Accountable?

Higher education's stakeholders are a varied group, including policymakers, alumni, students, staff, and faculty, and for public universities, the citizens of the state. Their expectations may differ greatly from each other, often putting boards in binds. In serving the public's interest, boards are accountable for their institution's mission and for the values that support the mission, including academic freedom, due process, and shared governance; academic quality; financial integrity; autonomy and self-regulation; transparency; diversity, equity, and inclusion; access and affordability; and service to the community. This list is a tall order. And boards do not get a "pass" on one dimension if they are succeeding in others. They must perform well across the different domains. We note five essential areas of board responsibility and accountability:

1. Mission: The board determines, upholds, and, when necessary, adapts the mission, including the institution's vision, purpose, guiding principles, programs, services, strategic plans, and priorities.
2. President: The board selects, compensates, evaluates, and fires the president. Increasingly, boards are also responsible for ensuring leadership succession plans are in place for the CEO and for other senior positions.

3. Finances: The board oversees the fiscal health and integrity of the institution, including (a) budget approval and adherence, (b) investments such as the endowment and reserve funds, and (c) the audit, which entails contracting with an independent auditing firm and overseeing its work. The board is also responsible for other assets, including the physical plant and real property. Importantly, members of the staff manage all of these areas, but the ultimate accountability rests with the board as it holds the president accountable for compliance and performance.
4. Programs and services: The board oversees the quality of institutional offerings. As with financial matters, staff and faculty members carry out the work, but the board plays an important oversight role to ensure the integrity and quality of curricular and cocurricular programs, activities, and services. Boards do this, in conversation with senior leaders, by setting measurable targets, benchmarking against peers, monitoring results, and holding the president accountable for institutional performance.
5. Board performance: The board is responsible for its own conduct; few can tell the board what to do or how to do it. In gross violations, regional accreditors or even the state attorney general may step in. However, for most boards, unfortunately, the old quip rings all too true: "When management screws up, the board fires the president; when the board screws up, the board fires president." But to have and maintain integrity, especially within a sector that values autonomy and self-regulation, it is essential for boards to be accountable for themselves.

Of this list, the final item tends to be the one boards most often are least prepared to carry out well and it may be the most difficult to manage. Ensuring board responsibility for its own conduct is the subject of the next section.

How Can Boards Ensure Governance Accountability?

So far, this all seems fairly straightforward. So why so many train wrecks? We don't believe they occur because laws, bylaws, and articles of incorporation aren't clear—they are. We don't believe they occur because of stupidity—by and large, trustees are smart, experienced people. We don't believe they occur because of evil intention—by and large, trustees want to do good work and serve faithfully. Perhaps they occur because it's easy to have words on paper, but more difficult to enact them. Some boards lack internal practices that help keep them aware of their accountability and that bring issues to light to help them avoid blind spots, potholes, and sinkholes. Other boards simply do not attend to this matter. They don't think of themselves acting in the sphere of public opinion and public scrutiny. That too is problematic.

We discuss here some good practices to ensure accountability for the board's performance by the board, but first a note about public institutions. Boards of public universities and state systems govern in public, which certainly ups the ante. State sunshine laws are intended to increase transparency and, correspondingly, accountability. But there's a downside too: Having to govern in public sometimes incents individual trustees to create workarounds or to curtail dialogue, robust discussion, provocative questions, and meaty deliberations.

All boards, whether governing in public or not, can serve their organizations better by ensuring accountability. We offer here some ideas about how.

Hold a Discussion About Board Accountability

Boards should periodically have a straightforward conversation about to whom they are accountable and how they might demonstrate it. Public boards may more easily have this conversation, given their appointment processes and the strong sense of priorities that exist in many states. Boards of independent colleges and universities may have a more complicated situation. Boards at religiously affiliated institutions may feel accountable to the sponsoring order. Other boards may identify other stakeholders such as students, alumni, donors, or the larger community.

The ways in which boards demonstrate accountability to each group may vary. Boards should outline the areas in which they need to be accountable and to whom. Topics such as financial stability, educational quality, performance management, oversights of and the advancement of assets, and presidential oversight and support are just some of the areas boards might explore. The more boards can be intentional about the "to whom" and "about what" of accountability, the better they will govern in both the short and long runs.

Practice Predecisional Accountability

In its simplest terms, this strategy means that trustees should make decisions as if they—not the president—had to explain them to stakeholders. This is one strategy to operationalize our first suggestion. For example, for each board meeting, randomly select two trustees who will, in mock trial fashion, need to explain board dialogue or decisions to an unknown entity (stakeholder group) waiting outside the door. Research has shown that groups practicing predecisional accountability increase engagement in dialogue, consider more stakeholder viewpoints (because they don't know who's waiting to hear the upshot), ask more questions, and take more notes; ultimately, when applied to boards—they govern better (Lerner & Tetlock, 1999, 2002).

Epitomize Performance Accountability for the Institution

If the board holds itself up as an exemplar of performance accountability, it is better positioned to hold others accountable as well as themselves. This means being explicit about the board's collective understanding of great governance, how it intends to execute it, and how it will measure it. Periodically (every two to three years, although some conduct an annual review) conduct a comprehensive self-assessment of the board's collective performance. It's also a good idea to have trustees self-assess their own engagement and performance. Although individual assessments might be a bit inflated, the simple act of self-reflection is helpful. It's also good practice to assess the work of committees and board meetings. Trower (2013) has provided additional specific ideas for all of these types of assessment.

Create and Uphold a Statement of Expectations

Another good practice is to have a written statement of trustee expectations, or a code of conduct, that spells out the responsibilities of board members and how the board will deal with violations. Make this statement public. Demonstrate that the board takes seriously the ways its members engage with each other and with the work of governance. It also helps boards moderate potentially disruptive behavior by a few rogue trustees. Great boards do not tolerate renegades who violate agreed-upon terms of engagement; there should be consequences for misbehavior, even when this is difficult for the board to carry out.

Seek Management's Overall Assessment Annually

The best boards engage in dialogue with the president about how the board is performing. Such conversations can happen with the board chair or with the executive committee and overarching views should be discussed with the full board. Some boards ask the senior staff members to also complete the written board assessment survey and analyze results comparing board to staff members, in the aggregate (so as to not compromise anonymity). Boards provide presidents with feedback and assessment, so why not reverse the process? This reverse process can be challenging given that boards hire, review, and fire presidents. But with this recognition, such an upward assessment can still be done meaningfully.

Hold Executive Sessions for Reflective Practice

In order to learn and improve, it is important for a board to reflect on its performance, which can often be best done in executive session without senior leadership present. Such sessions are a time for trustees to open up with each other about how they see the board's performance and talk about blind spots that may have been revealed in the assessments and how to overcome them.

Another best practice of effective boards is to periodically take stock of the past year and discuss both contributions/successes and shortfalls in terms of the board's governance function. What did we do especially well? Where did we fall short? Why? What have we learned? How will we govern still better in the year ahead?

Avoid Conflicts of Interest

This point should not need to be reinforced, yet trustees too often find themselves in conflict. Board accountability is undermined quickly and deeply when conflicts of interest exist. Although not all conflicts are avoidable, many are and should be. And for those in which there is a compelling benefit (Association of Governing Boards of Universities and Colleges, 2013), being transparent about those conflicts is important to board accountability.

Use the Mission as a Guidepost and Touchstone

Too many boards get into difficulty when their actions are viewed as running counter to the mission and values of the university. For example, boards lose credibility when they offer presidents excessive compensation packages, yet leave students with a high debt load or come under scrutiny for not paying staff living wages. Boards can charge trustees at each meeting to ask the probing question "How does this decision reflect on our values and mission?" Hopefully such a capacity will become naturally ingrained over time. This is a type of values "sniff test." If the decision smells bad, it likely is bad.

The Challenges of Accountability

Governance accountability is difficult for a variety of reasons. First, it often includes high-stakes decisions about which not everyone will agree. Furthermore, stakeholders are opinionated, and seemingly even more so given the easy access to social media. Second, board deliberations often take place behind closed doors or even if open without much of an audience. Third, many stakeholders don't understand governance and its role (see chapter 2 about the dynamics of governing today for additional discussion on this point). These factors add up to a degree of skepticism even if the board is doing its work well and honorably. Because of this, boards must work extra hard to ensure they are accountable.

Conclusion

In summary, there are many steps boards can take to ensure accountability for the board by the board. Because boards are at the apex of the organizations they serve, the buck stops with them. This fact creates challenges but also opportunities. They cannot and should not hide. And they should have nothing to hide. You may have noted an undercurrent running through all of this and that is integrity. Ultimately, board accountability boils down to integrity. Without it, nothing good can happen. Once violated, it is difficult to overcome. With it, good work is possible.

Questions for Boards

1. To whom is your board accountable? (Or to whom should it be accountable?) What evidence might you support to ensure accountability?
2. When is the last time the board had a discussion about accountability? To what extent is it time for a new one? How might the board hold regular discussions about accountability?
3. How well does the board assess itself and use the findings to improve its performance?
4. Does the board have a comprehensive and clear set of expectations for individual trustees? What is on that document? What should be on that document?

For Further Insight

To follow up on some of the issues raised in this chapter, we suggest:

- Chapter 2: The "Damned If You Do, Damned If You Don't" Dynamics of Governing
- Chapter 3: Is Your Board Mediocre?
- Chapter 6: Spending Scarce Time Wisely
- Chapter 8: Curiosity: The Boardroom's Missing Element
- Chapter 11: The (Not So) Hidden Dynamics of Power and Influence

8

CURIOSITY
The Boardroom's Missing Element

It's true that boards deliberate, provide answers, and engage in decision-making. But to do these things well, they must first be able to ask informed questions. Good boards ask good questions, but great boards ask great questions. What separates these two types of boards? We would argue an ingredient too often in short supply in boardrooms—curiosity. This chapter explores the notion of curiosity and how it can help boards ask the better questions that lead to better outcomes.

Questions Matter

The ability to ask meaningful questions is an important skill in the board-room and, we believe, fundamental to effective governance. Said the chairman of Bain & Company, Orit Gadiesh, in a 2009 *Harvard Business Review* interview, "The most distinguished board is useless and does a real disservice to the organization, in my view, if the people on it don't ask the right questions. If you're not asking questions, you're not doing your job" (Dowling, 2009).

But what constitutes a good question? "A beautiful question is an ambitious yet actionable question that can begin to shift the way we perceive or think about something—and that might serve as a catalyst to bring about change" (Berger, 2014, p. 8). In general, people avoid asking questions for four primary reasons: (a) questioning is seen as counterproductive (especially when it's answers that we seek, not more questions); (b) there never seems to be a good time to ask a question; (c) it's difficult to know the right questions to ask; and (d) people fear there may not be answers to the questions they pose (Berger, 2014).

Let's translate that to boardrooms where many trustees don't ask questions at all, let alone "beautiful" ones. Pronouncements, not questions, frequently carry the day. Why? Are there barriers to curiosity in the board-room? Unfortunately, there are many. Some boards develop a culture in which asking questions is perceived as an indication of incompetence. Advancing arguments or making statements—not inquiring—is rewarded and, thereby, reinforced. Questions are perceived to be the domain of the uninformed or the uninitiated. These boards prize the expertise of specific trustees who are often accomplished individuals in their own professions. These board members are recruited because they have answers or at least are perceived to have them. The culture of the board then reinforces this assumption. But boards are well served to recall the wonderful Frank Lloyd Wright 1957 quote, "An expert is someone who has stopped thinking because he 'knows'" (Popova, 2012).

In some boardrooms, presidents and staff don't readily welcome questions from trustees. "Let us explain to you what you need to know" is their modus operandi. In these boardrooms, staff drive board agendas and in turn look to provide answers. How many presentations have we all sat through as trustees only to find that we've run out of time for any substantive questions beyond a few seeking clarity on some small matter? In some instances, administrators minimize time allotted for asking questions because the board has a history of asking irrelevant questions and administrators learn to avoid potential cul-de-sacs to minimize their own headaches. In many ways, administrators share the responsibility for uninformed trustees because board orientation and ongoing board education are lacking, or because of an ineffective trustee vetting and selection process (but that is another story). In other situations, however, administrative leaders shoulder the blame because of their unwillingness to engage and share control of board meetings. Yes, this shared leadership can be risky, but it is a key ingredient for boards that add value. For no risk, they receive no reward, in terms of board contributions.

Finally, too often boards just don't have the proficiencies or the structures to foster curiosity. The agendas are overly full, the materials voluminous, and the discussions framed not to spur curiosity but rather to answer predetermined questions. (See chapter 6 on spending time wisely for more about effective board agendas.) Some boards focus on problem-solving or on oversight without an eye toward the future or strategy. Some boards do not intentionally make board education (which helps boards build the confidence and culture to inquire in meaningful ways) an intentional and ongoing part of the board's agenda. Boards that lack sufficient curiosity risk the following:

- Complacency and disengagement. It is too easy for the work of boards to become routine. Boards go through the motions of governance without the drive to really understand what they need to ask and discuss in order to govern well. When there is little investment in meaningful work, trustees—particularly busy, accomplished individuals—become disengaged.

- Lost opportunities to add value. Boards that lack curiosity foreclose occasions for trustees to meaningfully contribute. What are the contributions of boards, beyond philanthropy? Former secretary of labor Robert Reich (2013) once spoke publicly about his experience as a trustee, memorably noting, "We ate well." Such statements don't say much for the impact he felt the board had on that institution.
- Advocating answers to the wrong questions. Boards that don't develop the capacity for curiosity risk applying solutions regardless of the problems. Without understanding the real challenges, boards may pursue the wrong solutions.
- Falling short in their fiduciary duties. Boards that are not curious may be underperforming in their most fundamental responsibility: acting as a fiduciary. Without asking good questions, boards cannot effectively fulfill their duties of care, loyalty, and obedience (see chapter 1 on the ongoing evolution of boards).

On the flipside, curiosity in the boardroom can deepen engagement, intensify observation among board members of important issues, add diverse and better-informed perspectives to discussions, minimize trustee solutions in search of problems, and increase individual trustee fulfillment. Trustee curiosity can and should be encouraged, cultivated, and celebrated.

Boards can particularly benefit from a collective curiosity because trustees come from a variety of sectors and industries. Boards are composed of accomplished people, many of whom have learned over time how to ask impactful questions—a skill that is part of their success. The ability to ask and answer meaningful questions is how leaders get ahead, challenge norms, and find innovative pathways. The questions that a successful leader of a local bank has learned to ask over her career are in some meaningful ways different from those that are essential to a multinational manufacturing firm and from those asked by a successful tech entrepreneur. Because of this richness of backgrounds, boards can weave together these different ways of understanding and questioning to create a powerful approach to governing—one that yields deep and broad insight into higher education's complex issues.

Toward Better Decisions

Curiosity, which can be defined as "a desire to know, to see, or to experience that motivates exploratory behavior" (Litman, 2005, p. 793), can improve trustee engagement as well as decision-making, which is actually a complicated task to do well. Although people and groups make decisions multiple times every day, boardroom decision-making can be difficult. A common issue that impedes effective group decision-making is groupthink (Janis, 1973) "where a team of smart people ends up doing something dumber than they would have done on their own" (Sawyer, 2007, p. 66). With groupthink, in order to quickly achieve consensus, dissent is minimized (Grant, 2016), and decision-makers are unable to explore a variety of options (March, 1994).

Research also shows that groups tend to amplify the biases of individuals, not overcome them, particularly if the individuals in the group approach or frame the problem similarly (Sunstein & Hastie, 2015). In addition, groups as compared to individuals become more overconfident that their decisions are correct, and they are more likely to stay committed to a particular course of action even if it is failing (Sunstein & Hastie, 2015). None of these dynamics bodes, well for boards working in complex environments on nuanced and complicated issues.

Furthermore, as we discuss in chapter 10 on culture, group decision-making requires two mind-sets and stages. After groups determine what they are solving for (the purpose of the decision), they first need to identify the set of probable and possible choices. This is the identification phase (Sunstein & Hastie, 2015), which calls for divergent thinking where groups explore possibilities, maintain flexibility, and encourage imaginative approaches to address the agreed-upon problem. Second, boards must be able to shift approaches to identify an optimal solution (what Sunstein and Hastie call *selection*), which utilizes convergent thinking—the narrowing of choices—requiring comparison and an analytic systematic effort. As we argue in chapter 10, boards often have a strength or preference for either divergent or convergent thinking.

Curiosity can help with the myriad of challenges common to group behavior. Asking well-informed questions; bringing multiple perspectives to frame problems, challenges, or opportunities; and the ability to deliberate from different vantage points all benefit from curiosity. Even after the conclusion of the decision, the ability to be curious about the processes used and their potential vulnerabilities, as well as asking the "so now what?" part of decision-making, can be helpful.

How to Increase Curiosity in the Boardroom

Curiosity isn't simply an innate talent; it can be developed to help boards see challenges anew and make decisions with deeper insight. It can be cultivated intentionally among a collection of people if they take the following steps.

Break Routines

Too often board business is conducted in ways that eventually become routine, if not ossified. Routines are the enemy of curiosity. They create expected patterns of behavior that tend to elicit similar types of questions. If the board always conducts its business in one way, over time it learns the types of questions to ask and not to ask within that framework. Expectations rather than novelty shape the work.

By creating new routines in board and committee meetings, boards can spark innovation and curiosity. Seating trustees in small groups, rather than around the typical large board table, can spur different types of interactions and conversations. As one trustee said of this format, "I can look the other trustees in the eye." Holding board meetings off-site, such as at an innovative corporate headquarters, a high school, or a community center, can alter perspectives leading to new conversations. At one institution, a board "field trip" to the construction site of a new campus drastically altered a stalled conversation in two ways. First, the experience helped the board better understand the challenges and opportunities related to the types of academic programs that might be possible at the new campus. Second, it helped the board to think more deeply about the ways the institution might engage with the local community. Time spent actually walking through the community and the new building site helped the board approach its work differently. Furthermore, changing the order of reports and discussions or assigning different trustees to lead various sections of the agenda also can disrupt the commonplace.

Commit the Time

Routine becomes curiosity-killing unless it is designed to create opportunities that promote curiosity. Too often the agendas of board meetings are overly full and, therefore, overly scripted. Developing the time for reflection and discourse can encourage curiosity. Embedding board educational sessions as a continuation of board work can be powerful. Being judicious about the number of topics addressed in a board meeting and finding ways to "steal time" for probing questions are other strategies. Moving to consent agendas can help streamline routine board work. Limiting reports by staff members is another strategy to make time. Show-and-tell sessions with questions at the end don't leave much room for exploring new ground.

Take a Statement/Question Census

Some boards may believe that they are asking a significant number of questions. To check that assumption, charge someone with tallying the number of curiosity-driven questions asked over the course of a board meeting against the number of statements made and questions for clarification. The comparison will probably be telling. Some boards may need permission to be curious. Board leaders may need to not only ask for questions but also demonstrate curiosity themselves by raising an initial set of good questions.

Relabel Some Challenges as Puzzles

As scholar Spencer Harrison (2011) suggested in his work on curiosity in organizations, labels matter. He argued that issues framed as problems invoke a negative emotion and the search for solutions. Such work may foreclose curiosity. The same issue framed as a *puzzle*—and using that word or related terms—may lead to a mind-set geared toward exploration and divergent thinking. He argued that figuring out puzzles (and by extension, puzzling challenges) can be invigorating in ways that solving problems rarely are.

Craft Agendas as Questions

Many board meeting and retreat agendas are framed around a series of state-ments, when what the board really needs are questions. An agenda that is simply a list of topics—enrollment, campaign update, risk—as such doesn't create the expectation for questions and curiosity. In contrast, agendas posed as questions, such as the following from a board retreat, lead to curi-ous inquiry: What are the key trends in the regional economy and changing employment needs? How is the higher education marketplace changing in the region? What do we know about the next generation of students? What assumptions are embedded in our enrollment forecast and how will this affect the business model? How do we think about long-term sustainability? What ideas do we have for new revenue sources? (See chapter 6 on spending time wisely for additional perspectives on meeting agendas.)

Adopt Curiosity-Invoking Activities

Boards can leverage a set of small behavioral changes that can lead to new lev-els of curiosity. Practice matters. Before a particular agenda item, the board can engage in a 90-second brainstorm in which each trustee writes down a list of questions associated with the topic. Another powerful strategy is to ask trustees at the end of the board meeting to write down 1 question that they have when looking back at the board's work of that day. One can make a second request for each trustee to write down one question she or he had earlier in the day but didn't ask for a variety of reasons. The responses are col-lected and read back to the group. The "next generation" questions and the "unanswered" questions are ways to provoke and encourage curiosity. Not only that, but they shed light on the board's culture (chapter 10); what is unspoken and why are important indictors of group dynamics.

Understand Not All Questions Are Curious Ones

Boards often report that they are good at asking questions. And many are. The challenge is not the frequency of questions but the style and type of questioning. Some questions enable curiosity and openness, whereas others are simply interrogations. The latter are rarely helpful in moving conversations ahead. Questions such as "Why did you do that?" or "Didn't you consider X?" seldom spawn anything but defensiveness.

Roger Schwarz (2013), in a *Harvard Business Review* article, suggested the "You Idiot" test. He proposed that, when ready to ask a question, first ask yourself privately the question and add the phrase "you idiot" to the end. Why did the administration project the budget so poorly (you idiots)? Why did you not think students would protest (you idiot)? If the question sounds natural with that phrase at the end, it's not constructive.

Furthermore, some questions that trustees ask are merely rhetorical; others are posed not to expand the conversation but instead to place blame; others are intended to go unanswered because they are part of a soapbox or soliloquy by those who like to hear themselves talk. (And yes, this does happen in boardrooms.)

Strive for a Culture of Curiosity

Curiosity is contagious, and boards can create cultures where it flourishes. Developing the right culture—one that encourages constructive questions, that is defined by curious minds, that carefully and intentionally frames questions and appreciates the time and work required to engage this way—will serve boards well. Look at patterns of engagement. Who speaks and with what effects is an artifact of culture, for instance. Do discussions end when certain board members speak? Does the board expect constructive "devil's advocate" perspectives? Does it welcome devil's inquisitors? When is a consensus that is too easily reached questioned as being overly simplistic?

Invest in Board Education

Well-informed trustees ask well-informed questions. Boards that embed board education not only about trends in higher education but the big questions that institutions and their leaders are wrestling with can be insightful. Some boards conduct board education sessions at each board meeting; others set aside large portions of time at annual retreats. The goal of board education should not be to provide trustees with the answers but to give them the knowledge to ask insightful and well-informed questions.

About What Should Boards Be Curious?

Boards have much about which to be curious these days, including demographic trends; changing faculty work; student learning and degree relevance; student persistence and success; the intersection of access, affordability, and excellence; opportunities to grow revenue and new revenue streams; the impacts of technology on higher education and student learning; and many other issues. However, what might be most important is not the topic itself but the nature of the problem and the ability to grasp the complexities and opportunities behind the issues. It is impossible to discern and make meaning, as a group, without asking questions. Groups do not come to shared understanding of issues when individuals merely assert opinions.

Organizations and groups tend to face two types of issues: technical problems and adaptive challenges (Heifetz, 1994). Technical problems are those that are easy to spot and can be solved by applying current knowledge. They are well defined and widely understood. People are receptive to the proposed solutions and they can be easily implemented using the tools currently available within the organization. Technical problems may be easy or difficult to resolve, but the path forward is clear and understandable. Adaptive challenges, in contrast, are difficult to identify (and easy to deny), do not have "right answers," and are unsolvable with current skills and knowledge. The solutions and even the challenges themselves can be easily denied or resisted. They require new ways of conceptualizing the problem and new ways of working to address the problem.

The challenge, Heifetz argued, is that too frequently organizations treat adaptive challenges as technical problems, only to make matters worse. What looks like one type of problem may require that the work be reframed as an adaptive problem. In Table 8.1, we provide some comparisons of technical versus adaptive challenges relevant today.

Too often boards and leaders don't pause to ask how an issue might be framed, or reframed, or thought of in a different way that might lead to a different understanding and, in turn, a more effective approach to solving the problem. Developing the capacity for curiosity can help boards move beyond what might be initially framed as a readily solvable technical problem to understand the situation as a more complex and ambiguous adaptive challenge.

TABLE 8.1
Campus Issues as Technical Problems or Adaptive Challenges

Issue/Problem	*Technical Problems*	*Adaptive Challenges*
Sexual assault on campus	Rules and compliance problems	Institution's culture regarding risk and safety
Fund-raising down	Insufficient outreach	Mission no longer resonates
Website hits declining	Outdated Web architecture	Message no longer resonates
Faculty turnover	Faculty salaries	Quality of faculty work life
Excessive drinking	Poor alcohol policies	Harmful student culture
Student protest about race	Diversity numbers	Climate of inclusion and equity

One of us worked with a board to explore the technical and adaptive nature of the new president's top priorities for her first 18 months in office. Asking the board to think about how to frame each issue first as a technical problem and then as an adaptive challenge helped the board and the president identify different possible paths forward as well as blind spots that they had. This board, like so many others, was adept at identifying and framing technical problems. Framing the work as adaptive challenges was more difficult. This is a skill they agreed to continue to develop. Table 8.2 shows the president's top 6 priorities for examination as technical or adaptive, with space for the board to frame a technical and adaptive question for each.

The board can make helpful, specific contributions related to adaptive work when the problem facing the institution or board is not well understood, lacks a clear path forward, or does not have readily available metrics or milestones for progress. For each, boards can contribute the following:

- Understanding the problem. Adaptive challenges are defined by the lack of clarity, and even disagreement, around the true problem. Boards can play important roles in working with the administration to define the problem accurately. They can do this by asking clarifying questions and bringing new lenses to the situation.
- No clear path forward. Regarding this dimension of adaptive problems, boards can introduce new types of solutions. Since most trustees are from outside of higher education, they can offer ideas from other sectors and settings and help to translate, transfer, and test those ideas in the higher education setting. Although not all

ideas elsewhere will be readily adoptable, the insights trustees bring, coupled with a willingness to ask questions about the relevance of their ideas, can help forge novel solutions.
- No readily available markers of progress. Boards can also create the space for administrators and the campus to work on adaptive challenges. They can instill patience while also keeping attention on the issues. Furthermore, they can work with the administration on articulating milestones and metrics for success (see Figure 8.1).

TABLE 8.2
**A President's Top Priorities Examined Through
Technical and Adaptive Lenses**

Issue/Problem	Technical Problem	Adaptive Challenge
Enrollment growth		
New program development		
Articulating the unique student experience		
Campaign planning and preparation		
Developing a technology strategy and plan		
Adopting a one-campus model for online and campus-based programs		

Figure 8.1. The governance work of adaptive challenges.

Might not understand the problem	• Work to define the true problem(s) • Ask clarifying questions • Bring new lenses to the situation
No clear path forward	• Have patience • Introduce new sources of solutions • Translate, transfer, and test ideas
No readily available metrics or milestones for progress	• Help identify relevant metrics and viable milestones • Keep the spotlight on the issues

Conclusion

Boards that are intentionally curious develop deep investments in the institution and its trajectory. They create more rewarding experiences for individual trustees, are better strategic partners with the administration, challenge well-worn assumptions that may block progress, and bring their collective expertise to the problems (and puzzles) the institution faces.

Entrepreneur and innovator Elon Musk was quoted in an *Inc.* magazine article saying, "A lot of times the question is harder than the answer. If you can properly phrase the question, then the answer is the easy part" (Calhoun, 2017). Boards need to continue to develop the curiosity to pose and pursue just such questions.

Questions for Boards

1. How adept is our board at posing questions?
2. Are we a curious board or not? What evidence supports your answer?
3. What hinders and what would enable more curiosity?
4. What steps can we take to improve the culture for curiosity in our boardroom?

For Further Insight

To follow up on some of the issues raised in this chapter, we suggest:

- Chapter 5: Right Answers; Wrong Questions
- Chapter 6: Spending Scarce Time Wisely
- Chapter 10: The Culture of Boards: Making the Invisible Visible
- Chapter 13: Creating the Capacity for Trying Issues
- Chapter 14: Strategy, Higher Education, and Boards (and Forget Planning)
- Chapter 16: Governing Circa 1749

9

THE "JOBS" OF COMMITTEES

Of Drill Bits and Milkshakes

Much board work is done through various committee structures. Committees differ depending on the size of the board, the complexity of the institution or state system, the frequency with which the board meets, and the work to be accomplished. Regardless of the structure, each committee has tasks to accomplish. Unfortunately, too many boards are not sufficiently intentional about the work of committees and how one committee might work differently than another within the same board. We typically design the work of boards based on the tasks, or "jobs," each committee seeks to accomplish. And different committees present a mix of jobs. Knowing the mix of what jobs different types of committees can and should be doing can help boards better use their committees, stay out of the weeds, and remain focused on what matters most in terms of oversight and strategic imperatives.

The Work of Committees

Harvard marketing professor Theodore Levitt is said to have told his students, "People don't want to buy a quarter-inch drill. They want a quarter-inch hole" (Christensen, Cook, & Hall, 2005). The lesson he was conveying was not to focus on the tools or products (the drill bit), but to instead focus on the "job" people want to accomplish. With this same lens, we can focus on the jobs committees seek to accomplish to better understand their work and how it might be improved.

But first we explore committee structure, which seems to be a perennial issue for many board members and university leaders. (The focus tends to be on ensuring a breadth of drill bits rather than considering the needs for different types of holes.)

Committee Structure: Same but Different

Boards have a range of committees and different boards have different committee structures. There is no simple and consistent answer as to what is best. To make this more confusing, boards at similar institutions often have very different committees and committee structures, and dissimilar institutions may have similarly structured committees.

For example, let's compare the board committee structures of 2 large public institutions: the University of Cincinnati and the University of Michigan. The 9-person University of Cincinnati board (with 2 additional student trustees) has 7 committees governing its 44,783 students across 14 colleges and overseeing a $1.3 billion budget (see Figure 9.1). The 8-person University of Michigan board has just 3 standing committees governing 44,718 students across 19 schools and an academic health center and overseeing a budget of over $8.6 billion (see Figure 9.2).

Private colleges that are in many ways comparable can also have different committee and board structures, and in fact, they can have committee structures similar to very different public universities. For example, Skidmore College (New York) with its 2,613 students and 31 voting board members has 10 committees (see Figure 9.3). And another similarly sized, private institution—Cabrini University (Pennsylvania)—serves 2,150 students, has a board of 27 members, and has 6 committees, looking in some ways similar to public universities (see Figure 9.4).

According to the AGB (Association of Governing Boards of Universities and Colleges, 2016), most public boards have 6 committees and private universities have 8 committees, with research universities tending to have the most, on average, with 10 committees. (Michigan, with just 3, is an

Figure 9.1. University of Cincinnati board committee structure.

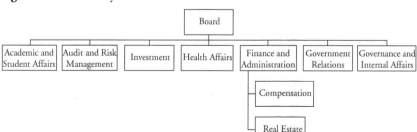

Figure 9.2. University of Michigan board committee structure.

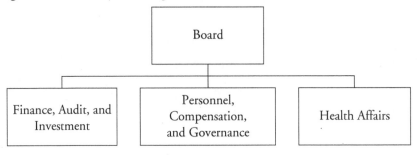

Figure 9.3. Skidmore College board committee structure.

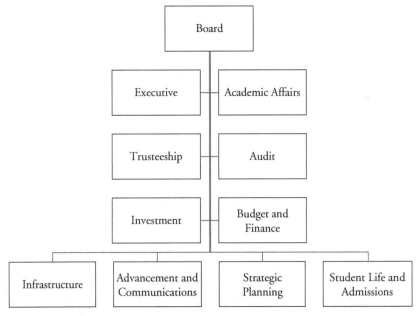

Figure 9.4. Cabrini University board committee structure.

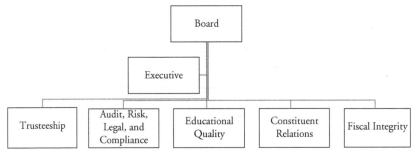

exception.) The most common committees are finance and budget, audit, academic affairs, and executive, for both public and private boards. The boards of private institutions typically also have a development or advancement committee, as well as a trusteeship or governance committee.

Most importantly, board size, institutional size, complexity, or mission need not drive board committee structure. Boards need enough committees to accomplish their work. No more, no less. But many boards simply continue, unexamined, with an historic committee structure, often institutionalized in bylaws. Some boards get locked into a discussion of structure without attention to purpose. (All drill bits and no holes.) These boards wonder, "Do we have too many committees? Too few? Are they the right committees?" Instead, they should ask, "What work do we need to accomplish through a committee structure? How can we ensure that the work of committees adds value?"

Right Topics; Right Committees

Looking at the substantive work that can be done in committees is more important than their number. The topics that committees tend to deal with include (a) money, how it is generated and spent (finance, investment, development, and audit); (b) the student experience both inside and outside the classroom (e.g., student affairs, academic affairs, or educational quality); (c) personnel, including compensation; (d) mission, especially at religiously affiliated institutions and government affairs for public universities and state systems; (e) infrastructure, particularly facilities but also technology and planning; and (f) the work of the board itself (governance, trusteeship, or nominating). Boards also create committees or task forces to focus on key university priorities such as athletics, commercialization and economic development, public-private partnerships, community relations, diversity, and academic health centers.

As boards evaluate their committees, they should try to answer certain questions:

- What important issues are not being sufficiently addressed by our present structure? How can we shift the focus of current committees or modify our committee structure to better address those issues?
- Do we have issue overlap or redundancy between committees?
- Are some committee agendas too full?
- Are some committees undertasked or consistently looking for work?
- What problems would restructuring help resolve? What problems might restructuring create?

Two factors drive committee restructuring efforts. The first is about *issues*—overlaps and gaps in how boards address specific topics, and the second is *workload*—overload or underload. The primary purpose of committees is to extend the board's capacity to look at issues more deeply by tapping the expertise of specific trustees. Committees typically do the legwork (go deeper) on complex issues within their purview and make recommendations to the full board; they help frame board-level discussions and facilitate better and more effective decision-making. Committees do some of the heavy lifting. The problem is that some board committees have too much to lift, whereas others don't have enough or know what to lift. And still other board committees are lifting the same things. (See Box 9.1 and Box 9.2.)

As one example, a strongly tuition-dependent private college (close to 85% of its revenue) found that issues of enrollment were discussed in both the finance and student affairs committees. However, both committees addressed issues of enrollment from different perspectives and would make decisions that often needed to be reconsidered by the other committee or when the topic reached the full board. This proved to be ineffective and inefficient. Because neither hand knew what the other was doing, the board found that it had an overlap problem. The solution was to create what started out as a board task force on enrollment that eventually morphed into a standing board committee (once the bylaws were updated).

Another tuition-dependent college board never talked about enrollment, although it was the primary source of revenue for the college and the college had a five-year history of uneven enrollment management. That board didn't recognize this structural gap in its work despite knowing it needed to give more attention to the issue. The structure of the committees and the

BOX 9.1.
Evolving Boards Mean Evolving Committees

One board that increased its size from 28 to 36 members found that it had to change from a board-centric format, where all members could easily discuss all issues, to a committee-centric arrangement. The increased size of the board meant that it was more difficult for everyone to speak at board meetings and that discussions of the full board were not as thorough as they had been previously. People became frustrated. Thus, the board had to shift to a stronger reliance on committees. This change not only affected how the board worked but also put new responsibilities on committee chairs to be much more active leaders—more intentional about committee agendas and outcomes—and the board had to place more trust in the committees and their chairs.

BOX 9.2.
Wheaton College's Restructuring

In 2015, Wheaton College (in Norton, Massachusetts) reconfigured its long-standing and somewhat siloed committee structure after an analysis of committee charters and work plans and a deep-dive discussion at a board meeting. That process about how to structure more efficient and effective board meetings yielded a single Educational Quality & Student Experience Committee where previously three committees (Academic Affairs, Student Affairs, and Faculty & Staff) had operated and a Reach & Reputation Committee where previously two committees (Advancement and Campaign Steering) existed.

traditional focus of the work in those committees meant that enrollment never received its needed board focus. It too created a board committee on enrollment but for a different reason—the gap it found in its work.

Relatedly, boards that rethink their committees often are responding to a recognition that their committees and the requisite work are misaligned. For some, the range or depth of issues the board must address has created an undue burden on its current committees (overload). Committee members find they can't get through their agendas sufficiently. For this reason, for example, some boards have pulled out issues related to technology from the facilities committee to create a new technology committee. Other boards have created committees or subcommittees related to real estate, removing that topic from the finance or campus planning committees.

Finally, some boards have discovered that committees that once were important simply do not have sufficient meaningful work to do today. In these cases, the board is bound by committee structures from yesterday's work and outdated bylaws. For example, some boards have struggled to find meaningful work for student affairs as their enrollments have shifted from traditional-age students to adult learners and the boundaries between student affairs and academic affairs has blurred (e.g., at one point, student development and assessment were student affairs issues; now, these topics are more firmly the purview of academic affairs). One Catholic college discovered that its mission committee struggled to find purpose and focus. (Yes, mission lacked purpose. Kind of unsettling or at least ironic.) It dissolved the mission committee and instead infused the mission work across its committees. It created a role akin to a "mission steward" (typically held by a member of the college's sponsoring order) on each committee, whose role was to ask mission-related questions and ensure that its standing committees each took on the values and mission conversation in their respective domains.

TABLE 9.1
Champlain College's Prior and New Committee Structure

Prior Committee Structure	Additional Focus Areas	New Committee Structure
Finance Committee Facilities Committee	+ Technology + People Center	Financial Sustainability Committee
Academic Affairs Committee	+ Student Life + Enrollment + Career	Student Experience Committee
Advancement Committee	+ Marketing + Strategic Communications	Engagement and Outreach Committee
Audit and Compliance Committee	+ Risk Management	Audit, Compliance, and Risk Management Committee
Committee on Trusteeship	None	Committee on Trusteeship
Executive Committee	None	Executive Committee
Compensation Committee	None	Compensation Committee

Champlain College approved an updated committee structure in 2018 to help ensure more effective oversight of core areas. They combined the Finance and Facilities Committees and augmented three others (see Table 9.1).

What matters most is not which structure to create, or to modify, but the work that needs to be done and how a board committee structure can fill gaps, address overlaps (issue-driven change), and deal with overload or underload (workload-driven change).

The Jobs of Committees

We return to the metaphor of the drill and the hole as it relates to committees. Some boards fall into the pattern (or trap) of approaching committee work in the same ways across different committees. (Imagine each committee as a one-eighth-inch drill bit). In reality, the work varies across committees, and a more nuanced understanding of the "jobs" different committees seek to accomplish might be helpful. First, more on the idea of "jobs."

Management professor Clayton Christensen and colleagues (Christensen, Cook, & Hall, 2005) provided the following illustration of Levitt's "jobs" idea.

It's about a milkshake. The authors described a firm that wanted to increase milkshake sales but struggled until they understood the "job" the drinker wanted to accomplish. The company was surprised first to learn that 40% of milkshake sales occurred in the morning. These consumers had, essentially, three jobs for those milkshakes: (a) consumable using only one hand while driving during long commutes; (b) more filling than doughnuts or other types of quick, easy-to-eat breakfast foods and less messy than bagels with cream cheese or jelly; and (c) providing a pleasant distraction while stuck in traffic. These are not the insights one typically has when thinking about milkshake sales. The company also discovered another quite different market segment— parents who were rewarding their children. These buyers purchased milkshakes for a different reason, so the strategies to increase sales for the morning customers (i.e., more fruit, thicker shakes, longer lasting, healthy) would not satisfy the "jobs" of the second group. Approaching milkshakes and the roles they fulfill in more traditional ways would not have opened the door to increased sales for either group and a single approach would have resulted in "a one-size-fits-none product" (p. 4). The company needed to understand the "jobs" the milkshakes were performing. This was not easy work and required creative thinking (and in this case, some inquisitive consultants as well).

Although boards are not in the milkshake business, there are some lessons from this example that are applicable to committees, particularly the "one-size-fits-none" notion. But first we return to our framework from chapter 1 (Table 1.2) about the work of boards that identified three types of activities—oversight (with a focus on the past), stewardship and problem-solving (a present focus), and strategy/problem-finding (with an eye on the future)—and the mind-sets required for each type of work—analytic, inquisitive, and exploratory (see Table 9.2).

This same framework can be applied to the work of committees; however, depending on that work, the "jobs" of the committees might be different. This framework can be helpful to understand committee work differences. The work of some committees by its nature is tilted toward accountability with its analytic mind-sets (e.g., the audit committee; see Figure 9.5), whereas other committees might focus more on strategy with an exploratory perspective (e.g., investment; see Figure 9.6). Finally, other committees (e.g., academic affairs; see Figure 9.7) might have an equal balance among the three types of work. The graphics illustrate the possible differences in the "jobs" committees might do.

With this understanding, boards may be better able to frame their committee work. They can understand the mind-set they need to bring to this work (analytic, inquisitive, or exploratory), and they can also understand that the jobs of one committee might be different from the jobs of another

TABLE 9.2
Board Work: The Past, Present, and Future

	The Past	*The Present*	*The Future*
Function	Oversight of progress/ Accountability	Problem-solving	Strategy/Problem-finding/ Mission guardian role
Mind-set	Analytic	Inquisitive	Exploratory
Sample questions boards ask	How did our actual performance compare with our budget projections? How well is our investment strategy working? Did the president have a successful year?	What is the cost of the new tuition and financial aid policy? Are we confident that students are learning? What are we doing about the academic performance of athletes?	What might X mean for our campus? What are the emerging trends in the economy to which we should respond?

Figure 9.5. The audit committee "jobs" emphasis.

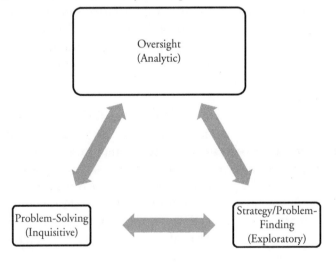

committee. For example, audit and finance. These committees may have some overlapping membership (those with financial and accounting expertise), but they also have different jobs to do and must do them differently. Audit likely spends little time on strategy (future-focused work), but the finance committee should.

Figure 9.6. The investment committee "jobs" emphasis.

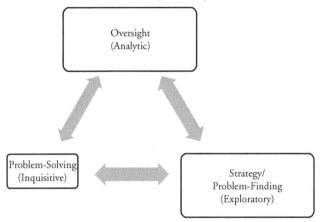

Figure 9.7. The academic affairs committee "jobs" emphasis.

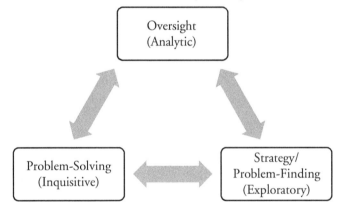

TABLE 9.3

**Committee Percentage of Time Allocated to Past,
Present, and Future (Current and Anticipated)**

	The Past	*The Present*	*The Future*
	Oversight of progress/ Accountability	Problem-solving	Strategy/ Problem-seeking
Percentage of time we are currently spending	____ %	____ %	____ %
Percentage of time we anticipate needing to spend	____ %	____ %	____ %

TABLE 9.4
Past Performance GPA for the Three Types of Work

	Oversight of progress/ Accountability (Mind-set: Analytic)	Problem-solving (Mind-set: Inquisitive)	Strategy Problem-Finding (Mind-set: Exploratory)
Performance GPA			

With these differences in mind, committees, much like boards, can reflect on the balance of their past work and discuss the desired balance moving ahead. Two tables repeated from chapter 1 (Table 1.3 and Table 1.4) might be useful for each committee both to discuss the amount of time they spend working in each category versus the amount of time they think they should be spending on each in the future (see Table 9.3) and to grade their performance (see Table 9.4).

Conclusion: The Three Cs of Committees

Finally, the work of committees is to support and advance the work of the board as a whole. To get the most out of committees, board leaders might keep three Cs in mind.

Coordination

Effective committees are well coordinated. They are coordinated internally through clear and intentional agenda planning (see chapter 6 for more discussion on meeting substance). Prior, proper planning regarding topics and a calendar for the next 12 to 18 months of committee meetings fosters coordination with other committees doing similar work and increases transparency to the full board about the upcoming work of the committee.

Collaboration

Boards that use their committees well are intentional about collaboration. They find ways to develop bridges between the related work of different committees. One board schedules a joint committee meeting of the enrollment and finance committees to discuss enrollment targets and their financial implications. Another board intentionally writes into its committee charges an overlap of technology responsibility between its academic affairs and buildings and grounds committees.

Another element of collaboration is to invite visitors and resource people to committee meetings. Broadening the number of voices in committee discussions can be helpful. For example, inviting faculty to participate in different aspects of academic or student affairs meetings or to provide input into board conversations about diversity creates a collaborative environment and helps the board do its work.

Communication

The final element is communication. Committees that are intentional about communicating not only the outcomes of their work but also the factors that they considered in their deliberations foster better governance. Too often the work of committees is done behind closed doors (or concurrently when other committees are meeting) and the richness of the discussion is not easily communicated. Boards often assume that individuals who sit on different committees will naturally convey what happened in one committee to another. This is not always the case. Being deliberate about communicating committee work and decisions is needed as people often quickly move from one meeting to the next.

The work of the three Cs is the responsibility of committee chairs because they set the agendas, liaise with university administrators, and are responsible for facilitating well-run meetings that lead to meaningful discussions.

Questions for Boards

1. When was the last time we examined our committee structure?
2. Is our committee structure serving us well?
3. What's the work that needs to be done?
4. Does our committee work align well with strategic institutional priorities?
5. Do some committees have too much work? Not enough work? Are there redundancies?

For Further Insight

To follow up on some of the issues raised in this chapter, we suggest:

- Chapter 1: The Evolving Board: Ways to Think About Governing Today
- Chapter 3: Is Your Board Mediocre?
- Chapter 5: Right Answers; Wrong Questions
- Chapter 11: The (Not So) Hidden Dynamics of Power and Influence

---

IO

THE CULTURE OF BOARDS
Making the Invisible Visible

Governing boards are dynamic groups of individuals where, sometimes, the whole does not equal the sum of the parts. Presidents want and need their boards to be active, productive, and engaged assets for the university, college, or state system they govern, yet too many boards, as collectives, underperform. Educating boards on *what* they should do—their roles and responsibilities—although important, is insufficient. Underperforming boards may know their roles but have cultures that limit their effectiveness. Board culture, those patterns of behavior and ways of understanding that are deeply engrained, reinforced, and taught to new trustees, is what demands attention. It has been said that culture eats structure and strategy for lunch, and we agree. But culture is much more elusive and difficult to explain succinctly, making it a challenge to expose and to leverage constructively.

Board Dynamics Matter

Governing boards are groups of people whose inner-group dynamics matter in terms of overall performance. We have seen the worst: disengagement; inner circles and power cliques; less than candid conversations; distrust and disrespect among trustees or between the board and management; inappropriate behaviors by individual trustees; and uneven distribution across trustees of information, airtime, and influence. It's impossible for a board to govern effectively as an ineffective group. These obstacles to excellent governance are not removed through bylaw revisions, reconfigured committees, or changes in the frequency or duration of board meetings. These are matters of board culture, not structure or procedure.

Culture is difficult to define; however, a description is helpful as we consider the cultural norms of boards. "Culture is the tacit social order of an organization: It shapes behaviors in wide-ranging and durable ways. Cultural norms define what is encouraged, discouraged, accepted, or rejected within a group" (Groysberg, Lee, Price, & Yo-Jud Cheng, 2018, p. 46). It also is difficult to measure and discuss, so trustees often hesitate to examine thoroughly the board's chemistry, behaviors, and norms.

And it's more difficult still to change these dynamics. Until now. We present a field-tested means to diagnose and categorize board culture that distills important insights and implications from data and enables trustees and senior staff to explore how they might leverage board culture for the better. When the board's culture improves, the board's performance improves, and the institution is better served.

The Silent Director

The focus on board culture is based on the premise that it is not *what* boards do (or don't do) but *how* trustees think and interact while governing that really matters. Most boards function sufficiently (we argue they are "striving for mediocrity" in chapter 3); they go about their business, and the institution goes about its work. But the best boards function in ways that add value to the institutions they serve. (There are, of course, boards that operate at the other end of this continuum, and we read about them in the newspapers, but this chapter is not about serious dysfunction.) An important differentiator between the majority of boards—those simply mediocre—and those that add significant value isn't their structure or size, the tenure of their leaders, or the frequency or lengths of their meetings; it's *how* they work together (Chait, 2016; Charan, 2005; Prybil, 2006).

In the first chapter, we have defined *board culture* as those patterns of behavior and ways of understanding that are deeply engrained, reinforced, and taught to new trustees. Because of its importance in how culture affects trustee interaction and board performance, it demands attention.

Boards are complex and sophisticated social groups. They have their own dynamics that propel or impede their collective impact. As Yale's Jeffrey Sonnenfeld (2002) noted, the path toward better board performance is "to manage the social system a board actually is" (p. 106). It is this social system that is often left unattended. "Most directors aren't aware of the group dynamics that affect the board's behavior . . . how much their membership in groups influences their behavior and how others behave toward them" and are, therefore, "blind to the need to correct it in some cases or to exploit it in others" (Alderfer, 1986, p. 38). Attempts to improve governance through policy mandates, better information, and restructuring committees address only part of the problem and may never get at the core of ingrained patterns of behavior that really matter to board effectiveness. "Changes in structure and operations have produced greater efficiency, but problems like disengagement, dysfunction and misconduct persist—challenges that alterations to board architecture and mechanics cannot resolve" (Chait, 2016, p. 20). Board culture matters—so much so that it has been called "the invisible director" (Alderfer, 1986, p. 38). But here is the difficult part: Culture is often invisible to those immersed in it and therefore difficult to make concrete and actionable. The challenge is to make culture visible so that it can be changed when it gets in the way of effective governance.

Defining *Organizational Culture*

As noted, organizational culture is an ambiguous concept, both in terms of definitions and one's ability to capture it easily. Appropriate to our focus on board dynamics and how new trustees become enculturated, *culture* can be defined as follows:

> A pattern of shared basic assumptions that the group learned as it solved its problems . . . that has worked well-enough to be considered valid and, therefore, to be taught to new members as the correct way to perceive, think, and feel. (Schein, 1992, p. 12)

There are several ideas important for boards as they think about their culture, including the following:

- Culture is developed within each group and therefore unique to that group. Understanding culture at a meaningful level is not about fitting board cultures into set categories or typologies. Although boards are likely to share some similarities in their cultures, there are cultural specifics to each board.
- Culture continually evolves. Because culture is based on learning through experience, as the experiences change and new lessons are learned, culture can evolve and be changed as well. In addition, as new members join boards, the cultural dynamic also changes because newcomers alter the team.
- Culture includes a range of ways of understanding and responding. It shapes the ways that board members make sense of events, develop

consensus about which types of questions are appropriate to ask and not to ask, and determine patterns of influence of who speaks with what authority.

- Culture is transmitted to new board members. Intentionally or unintentionally, new members of a board learn its culture over time. It only takes one time to ask the wrong question or challenge the wrong person to learn (the hard way) the rules of the game. Therefore, astute new board members often become aware of the implicit dimensions of a board's culture before they become enmeshed in it.

Making Culture Visible and Actionable

To make board culture—which mostly comprises "unconscious group processes" (Alderfer, 1986, p. 38)—manageable and understandable, we have identified a set of cultural dynamics applicable to the boardroom. We sought elements that can be framed as continuums to be able to create cultural profiles of boards. The point is not to determine a good and bad culture, but to describe board culture in concrete ways and facilitate board discussions about the strengths and potential vulnerabilities of that cultural profile for that particular board at this point in time.

Our continuum elements, discussed in more detail in the following paragraphs, include the diffusion of influence, decision-making tendencies, dominant mind-sets, and a challenge/support bias. There are also important issues of comportment—trust, respect, and candor. Board culture may very well consist of many factors (see chapter 1, Table 1.1); however, to make culture concrete, measurable, actionable, and comparable, we identify the following discrete set of elements that have risen to the fore in focus groups, interviews, and research on the topic of what matters most to measuring board culture.

Patterns of Influence

Power dynamics influence how groups of all types function (Baldridge, 1971; Raven, 2008). The sources of that influence may be tied to a variety of power bases (French & Raven, 1959). It is not uncommon, for instance, for wealthier board members to have extra influence because of their philanthropic potential or for longer-serving trustees to have influence due to experience. (See chapter 11 on power within boards for more discussion of the sources of these board dynamics.) However, the question regarding board culture is "To what extent is power consolidated in the hands of a few versus widespread among board members?" This dimension of culture influences how boards, as a group, act.

Decision-Making Preferences

Boards use their collective judgment to decide, offer suggestions, and help leaders think in different ways. The question we pose is "How well does the board, as a group, *decide?*" To make decisions, boards must do two things: identify the list of potential solutions, which requires flexibility and imagination (Sunstein & Hastie, 2015), if not foolishness (March, 1994), and select the preferred solution, which requires groups to be "tight and analytic" (Sunstein & Hastie, 2015, p. 15). These are two different processes. Boards may have a preference for deciding in ways that are "fast" (intuitive and emotional) or they may have a preference toward decision processes that are "slow" (calculating, logical, and deliberative) (Kahneman, 2011). The way boards think about problems may be to diverge (the messy, complex first step) or it may be to converge (the tight, analytic process). We classify a board's decision-making tendency as convergent or divergent thinking.

Mind-Set

The composition of most boards consists primarily of individuals who are not of the academy. They are lay trustees who come from a variety of professional backgrounds, the most common being corporate (Association of Governing Boards of Universities and Colleges, 2016). Yet these are individuals who have made a commitment to the academic ideals of their universities and colleges (Association of Governing Boards of Universities and Colleges, 2015b; Drucker, 1990), work closely with academic leaders, and engage with faculty and students. They walk the line between their day jobs and their academic volunteerism. These two worlds—with their different *mind-sets*—affect board culture. Associated with each are different assumptions about what leaders do, the role and prerogative of faculty, and the impact of mission, for instance. Mind-sets matter regarding how boards understand and act. Mind-sets create lenses which call into focus some things and minimize others (Gioia & Thomas, 1996; Weick, 1995). Does the board have a disposition toward a corporate mind-set or an academic one?

Challenge and Support

How boards perceive their roles may come down to their assumptions regarding support or challenge (Boyd, Takacs Haynes, & Zona, 2011). Although greatly oversimplifying their work, some boards believe their primary role is to manage risk, ensure compliance, and keep the university or college on track (Pearce & Zahra, 1992). This is the challenge function. Other boards see their role as that of stewardship, in which they act in the best interest of the institution, tilting their behavior toward cooperation, collaboration, and support (Westphal, 1999). This fundamental belief in one role or the other shapes how boards approach their work, set their priorities, and favor some issues over others.

Comportment

Finally, how people treat each other is a fundamental component of board culture. Factors such as trust, candor, and respect contribute much to the prevailing tenor in all types of work groups (Cerna, 2014; De Jong, Dirks, & Gillespie, 2016). These elements work in concert to reinforce each other, leading to more beneficial outcomes. "Positive expectations about others facilitate positive behaviors when interacting with them; those behaviors, in turn, strengthen positive expectations; hence, a virtuous cycle in which expectation and action collude to create and reinforce desired outcomes" (Kramer, 2010, p. 83). Trust, candor, and respect are essential to board behavior. Unlike the issues noted previously, this one is not a continuum. More trust, candor, and respect are always better in a boardroom than less of each.

Putting the Pieces Together

Board cultures are complex composites of the characteristics and preferences noted previously. To make sense of this information and organize it in a way that is helpful, we borrow an idea from a popular personality framework— the classic Myers-Briggs Type Inventory. This inventory helps individuals understand their preferences along a continuum and the strengths and weaknesses of those preferences (Quenk, 2001). For example, being introverted or extraverted, on its face, is neither good nor bad; rather it depends on the context and the ways in which strengths and blind spots play themselves out for an individual. We believe a similar approach can help boards understand their culture, their strengths, and potential vulnerabilities, and then act upon those understandings to improve governance.

The one exception, as noted previously, relates to comportment. Having more trust between board members is better than less, having more respect for one another and each other's contributions is healthier then animosity, and being more open is more desirable than having off-line conversations or

Figure 10.1. Dimensions of board culture.

How boards act	• Consolidated versus Distributed Influence
How boards decide	• Convergent versus Divergent Thinking
What mind-set boards have	• Academic versus Corporate
How boards perceive their role	• Partner versus Critic
How individuals treat each other	• Trust, Respect, and Candor

so-called parking lot meetings (discussions that occur after the board meeting as trustees head to their cars).

For the dimension of culture described previously we have developed continuums, shown in Figure 10.1. For each dimension, we identify cultural strengths and potential vulnerabilities, some of which we outline in the following sections. The strengths are elements that the board might leverage to further advance governance. The vulnerabilities are those elements to help them take stock of potential shortcomings and develop strategies to respond. The point of all of this is, again, to make culture explicit and actionable, with the intent of helping boards govern better.

A Profile in Action

We developed a survey to reveal a board's "cultural profile." The following example is from a private university (alias Mid-South University) with a board of 27 trustees. The italicized sections of each part of the continuum are its "profile"—in this case, distributed influence, divergent thinking, corporate mind-set, and partner role (see Figure 10.2). The percentages indicate how strong or consistent the board's preference is for each element. For example, in terms of comportment—trust, respect, civility, and candor —Mid-South scored very well (see Figure 10.3).

For each dimension, we outline examples of strengths and potential vulnerabilities, which become topics of conversation for a board retreat. Examples of the upside and potential drawbacks of boards with Mid-South University's profile may be found in Tables 10.1 through 10.4. These positive and potentially negative aspects for each element in an institution's profile provide a springboard to get the board discussing how it sees each play out in the boardroom.

Figure 10.2. Mid-South University culture profile.

	Consolidated Versus *Distributed* Influence	
Influence	35%	65%
	Convergent Versus *Divergent* Thinking	
Thinking	23%	77%
	Academic Versus *Corporate* Mind-Set	
Mind-set	44%	56%
	Partner Role Versus Critic	
View Role	60%	40%

Figure 10.3. Mid-South University comportment scores.

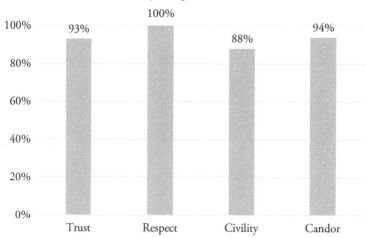

The story of board culture and its impact on the dynamics for Mid-South University's board go beyond these elements, however. For example, when we examined the responses of women trustees, we learned that they had very different experiences from their male counterparts regarding consolidated/distributed influence (see Figure 10.4).

Women trustees reported patterns of consolidated influence rather than the distributed influence reported in the main. This reveals a blind spot for the male trustees. Whereas the men reported that the board treated everyone and their ideas equally, the women reported experiencing power dynamics

TABLE 10.1
Distributed Influence Strengths and Potential Vulnerabilities

Strengths	Potential Vulnerabilities
Many (potentially diverse) opinions shape discussions and decisions	May slow decision-making
Benefit from broad and diverse perspectives	Arguments and disagreements may not be resolved
When certain individuals are absent, the work can continue	May become the "Wild West" when focus is necessary
Minimizes an "in group" on the board	Uninformed, but vocal, members may have too much influence
More people feel that their input matters	
Contributes to feelings of connectedness to the board and its work	

TABLE 10.2
Divergent Thinking Strengths and Potential Vulnerabilities

Strengths	Potential Vulnerabilities
Intentionally welcomes diverse opinions	Difficulty zeroing in on the key issues and a course of action
Well suited for complex issues	Little easy consensus among trustees
Focuses on exploring problems	Trustees may feel they are not on the same page
Minimizes the potential for blind spots	May make it difficult to "pull the trigger" on some decisions
Fosters "creative" problem-solving	May result in the board overthinking certain problems

that rested in the hands of a few. They saw a "board within a board" that the men who sat in the most influential positions did not see. Through a facilitated discussion, the board came to recognize that the key committees were male-dominated, that the executive committee was all male except for its newest member (who reportedly "doesn't say much"), and that the committee recommendations that the board seemed to revisit and doubt the most were those coming from the handful of committees where most of the women served. The male chairs and their committees were rarely, if ever, second-guessed by the board.

TABLE 10.3
Corporate Mind-Set Strengths and Potential Vulnerabilities

Strengths	Potential Vulnerabilities
Brings "discipline" to board work and the institution	Views mission as a tool (strategy), rather than having intrinsic value
Uses data to drive decisions	May not attend to academic values; overemphasizes bottom line
Favors management tools (key performance indicators)	May value the immediate and new over long run and historic
Focus on the financial bottom line	May not appreciate shared governance or faculty voice (don't see faculty as partners in shaping strategy)
Market matters; strive for responsiveness to customers and competition	May overvalue administrative view and undervalue faculty opinion
Bias toward leadership at the top; reinforce presidential prerogative	Could wade into areas without realizing the weights of their questions (program closure; tenure)

TABLE 10.4
Partner Role Strengths and Potential Vulnerabilities

Strengths	Potential Vulnerabilities
Focus on the institution first and not representing stakeholders	Does not ask hard or unpopular questions
Easily "partners" with president	May follow administration's lead too easily
President shares challenges openly	May give up ownership of agendas (board and committees)
Better, more comprehensive information flow between board and administration	Responds rather than shapes or drives
Staff work openly with committees	May easily blur governance and management

The board made the following changes after surfacing this cultural rift. It agreed to rethink its process for appointing committee chairs and worked to assign women to the more influential committees, such as finance and academic affairs. The board chair and committee chairs became more

Figure 10.4. How women versus men view influence (consolidated versus distributed) at Mid-South University.

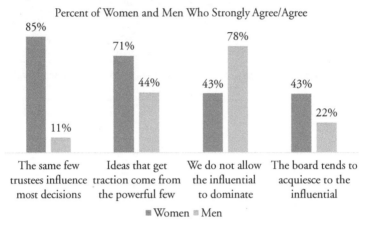

Percent of Women and Men Who Strongly Agree/Agree

cognizant about who speaks and who does not, and now intentionally structure discussions that seek input from those individuals who are often quiet in deliberations. This board was willing to change its patterns of influence once it realized this hidden dynamic. But other boards are not as willing to challenge the status quo regarding power dynamics (see chapter 11 for more discussion).

The "cultural profile" also allows the consideration of the interactions of different cultural components or how they work as a set. For instance, divergent thinking coupled with distributed influence is likely to help the board think broadly about complex issues and not rush to conclusions before they understand the issue from multiple perspectives. The partner role coupled with the corporate mind-set might suggest that the board has an ability to understand this particular university and how it is situated in the higher education sector, and have the discipline to stay focused on key performance metrics without becoming overly enamored by mission. Such a board can appreciate both mission-based performance metrics as well as those related to financial viability. The cultural profile of Mid-South University points clearly to strengths that the board can more intentionally leverage as it operates, provides a set of descriptors about how it works to help new board members transition onto the board, and reveals blind spots for the board to address.

Context Is King

As with most things, when it comes to culture, context is important. Although others may suggest that there is a better, if not best, board culture, we think that context matters. This is the reason we identify strengths and potential vulnerabilities for each dimension (except comportment, as we've noted). For example, distributed influence is not always better or healthier than consolidated influence. Think about a very large board, in a highly dynamic situation or in crisis mode, where it needs to make decisions quickly. This board, and its president, may be well served by a board culture that has consolidated influence. A small number of highly respected and good board leaders are able to respond quickly. They do their homework and are well informed about complex issues and have the trust of the president and the rest of the board. However, consolidated influence may create vulnerabilities. A board that has consolidated influence functioning in a different context may benefit from widespread input to understand novel and complex situations. That board may find itself excluding well-informed members who have much to add. If a small group of trustees dominates all board work, takes up the most airtime during board meetings, shapes all agendas, and even talks over other trustees, why would others participate? What is important is the strengths and vulnerabilities in light of the work the board needs to conduct and the context in which it operates.

Conclusion

A cultural lens to the work of boards can shed light on many important factors. But the real benefit is having the means to make elements of culture visible and thus actionable, not simply saying culture matters. What boards do with the information about their culture is what matters most. Once boards have the language to understand their own culture, the subsequent work should focus on the extent to which the board's culture is aligned with the demands of the environment in which the institution and the board has to work and the nature of the work it faces. The cultural profiles of boards suggest that they may be well suited for some work and some situations, but ill-prepared for other situations. Knowing these can be extremely important to ensure ongoing board effectiveness.

Helping the board and the president understand the board's strengths and blind spots is essential to make culture actionable. This process allows the president and board members to have meaningful conversations about the operative board culture, determine whether it is working well in the current (and future) context, think about what changes to culture might be helpful, and develop strategies to act. The board culture profile provides a road map to align board dynamics with the work the board needs to accomplish, the president's leadership style, and the institution's context.

The real goal of understanding board culture and its influence on how boards work can put governance on the pathway toward increased effectiveness. It is making sure that "invisible director" is moving the board in the right direction.

Questions for Boards

1. How much thought have you given to the role culture plays in your boardroom?
2. What are some words that might describe your board's culture? How consistent do you think these descriptors would be across the trustees? Would you identify the same words or different ones?
3. What strengths and potential vulnerabilities do you see in your current board culture?
4. Do you have the right culture for the context in which you are operating and the work the board is facing?

For Further Insight

To follow up on some of the issues raised in this chapter, we suggest:

- Chapter 1: The Evolving Board: Ways to Think About Governing Today
- Chapter 3: Is Your Board Mediocre?
- Chapter 5: Right Answers; Wrong Questions
- Chapter 11: The (Not So) Hidden Dynamics of Power and Influence
- Chapter 15: Getting to Grips With Shared Governance.

II

THE (NOT SO) HIDDEN DYNAMICS OF POWER AND INFLUENCE

B ecause boards are groups of people, social dynamics come into play. An important dynamic is the balance, or imbalance, of power within the board. Power comes from a variety of sources in the boardroom, including the obvious—experience, knowledge, and expertise—but also, and less obvious, participation, information, and the ability to control rewards and coercion (think philanthropy). Understanding the sources and balance of power is a window into explaining much about how boards behave and the outcomes they achieve.

Power in the Boardroom

Because boards sit at the top of the organization, and the president serves at the pleasure of the board, boards are powerful; they have legal, legitimate authority for decisions. In other words, the buck stops with the board. Beyond this institutional power, there is another power dimension at play that derives from the individual trustees themselves and how they interact with each other and with the president and the institution. These power dynamics greatly shape how boards behave, who has influence, the source of that influence, how it is wielded, and whether it is balanced among board members or consolidated in the hands of a few.

Boards for the most part are composed of people of influence. Public boards are political appointments and, by definition, tend to be influential in their states and regions. Private boards select their own members, often looking for accomplished and thus influential people. Put these individuals in a room together, and you are guaranteed some degree of power dynamics because many are used to calling the shots. Power and its dynamics are well recognized (people know who the power brokers are on the board) yet little understood regarding how it shapes board behavior.

This topic begs an initial question: Is it possible to foster effective collaboration necessary for good governance across power dynamics? The quick answer: Not really. A couple of factors contribute to this challenge. First, according to the research on groups, those which comprise powerful and influential individuals may be somewhat predestined for ineffectiveness. Yes, ineffectiveness. Groups of high-performing and influential individuals (which most boards have) often perform poorly together, whereas each performs well as individuals. Hildreth and Anderson (2016) wrote, "Despite the performance benefits power can provide when individuals work alone, at the group level, the possession of power might disrupt group processes and, thus, dampen collective performance" (p. 262). Their research shows that groups of powerful individuals are less likely collectively to focus enough time and attention on group tasks and instead are more likely to pursue their own interests and agendas, even at the expense of group progress. Highly influential individuals are used to pursuing their own agendas, not collaborating as peers. Other research (Sleesman, Conlon, McNamara, & Miles, 2012) suggests that these types of people are more likely to resist changing course or considering new approaches because of their track records of success along with feeling that their reputations are on the line. Powerful groups are blinded by success and by status. It seems too much power, even spread across the group, can be detrimental to its work. "While the possession and experience of power can make individuals more capable than others on individual tasks, that same power appears to undermine their ability to get along and work with each other on collaborative tasks" (Hildreth & Anderson, 2016, p. 282).

A second group performance barrier related to power is that boards frequently have uneven levels of power and influence within their ranks. If the board does not completely comprise highly influential people, then it has some who are more influential than others. This imbalance may also contribute to lower performance. (Sensing a damned if you are, damned if you are not situation.) Research from Hildreth and Anderson (2016) shows that "a group's performance depends on whether its members cooperate with each other, communicate effectively, and put selfish interests aside for the good of the collective" (p. 261). When power is consolidated in the hands of a few, cooperation, selflessness, and open communication may be lacking and group performance suffers as a result. The most powerful individuals "can become overconfident in their own ideas, devalue the performance of others and take credit for others' contributions, become more self-focused and less concerned about others' welfare, become less polite, interrupt and speak out of turn, and take others' opinions into account less" (p. 262). None of these bode well for board performance.

Boards thus face one of two problems: Boards of equally powerful people lack collaboration and are dominated by power standoffs (and egos) that impede group processes, or boards with unequal power have individuals who become overconfident in their own ideas, dominate discussions, disrupt, and don't listen. Either way, the result is lower performance. Or maybe we just need boards where no one is influential and accomplished? Pick your problem.

As we explore in this chapter, the situation is not completely dire. Boards can become more effective at group work by understanding the different sources of power, knowing how power manifests itself in the boardroom, and taking steps to manage power and its influence.

The Foundations of Power

Before we completely give up on boards, it is useful to know a bit more about power in organizations and groups and its sources of influence. The classic framework, offered by French and Raven (1959), outlines a series of bases from which power stems. They postulate the following bases of power (originally noted as five but updated to six; see Raven, 2008):

1. Information: power derived from having certain knowledge or information or access to that knowledge. Think about board members who have insider information from the president or governor versus those who do not.
2. Reward: the ability to influence behavior through positive incentives. For example, consider the influence of wealth in boardrooms and those able to reward the university through philanthropy (sometimes a criterion for the board chair position).
3. Coercion: threatening through penalties or negative consequences if someone does not comply or just the risk of rejection or disapproval from an admired person. Do some board members threaten to withhold donations if they don't get their way?
4. Legitimacy: power that comes from an organizational position. The power we give board chairs or committee chairs due to their positions.
5. Expertise: that influence of an individual based on superior insight or knowledge about a particular topic. The power that certain trustees can wield based on their knowledge and skills. For example, consider the

influential position of an accountant on the audit committee, an investment banker on the finance committee, or a real estate developer on the facilities committee.

6. Reference: power that stems from an individual wanting to be like the person of influence. We sometimes see new board members adopt the attitudes and approaches of those individuals whom they see as influential on the board.

Others have added to this list other sources of power in organizations and groups (Bolman & Deal, 2017); for example, the following sources of power are particularly relevant to boards:

- Alliances and networks: access to networks and the ability to build collaborations to get things done. Board members who can tap extensive professional and personal networks to advance the interests of the board. Who on the board has strong ties to the governor?
- Personal: power stemming from individual characteristics that lead to influence such as charisma, elocution, vision. How many board members "light up a room?"

Board members and presidents are keenly aware of where power lies among the trustees. What they may not know are the different sources of power and how those sources create certain board dynamics.

A caveat about power. It is important to note that power is not a negative in organizations or within groups. We often talk of "power plays" in organizations or look poorly on the politics that inevitably stem from power and influence. Thus, the idea of power tends to invoke unfavorable reactions. Power is on its own not bad; it is neutral until it is invoked. And at that point, power can be used for progress or disruption. Power can be put to good uses, and it often is in boardrooms. Powerful people, on boards as well as generally in life, can get things accomplished, call attention to certain issues, and ensure that decisions are implemented. We rely on power for progress. *Influence* is a seemingly gentler term, but it is not much different from *power*. Influential individuals are able to sway thinking or drive ideas because they have various levers of power at their disposal. We want boards comprising well-meaning individuals (remember those duties of care, loyalty, and obedience?) to leverage their sources of power positively to work on behalf of the university or state system. We want people with strong networks, individuals with expertise, philanthropists, and even charismatic people to help us get things done. Power is important to governance.

Everyone likely knows of situations where power has been used for the wrong objectives, damaging institutions and impeding boards. A frequently acknowledged issue in boardrooms is that big donors or deeply networked trustees are overly influential. However, the source may not be the problem. How and for what ends individuals with access to sources of influence use them may matter more. If those influential individuals are wonderful team players who work tirelessly on behalf of the college or university, few are concerned with the source of their influence. If these individuals tap their sources of power for personal gain or to be disruptive, people notice.

Lack of power also impacts boards. We've had conversations with individual trustees (privately) who express frustration with their inability to influence the board. In some instances, their perspective is well grounded and they could contribute much to board work, but the sources of power that determine who speaks, about what, and with what effect are not the ones they can tap. However, other individuals report the same frustration with lack of influence but don't have expertise, are unable to provide needed information, do not have the networks or alliances to move the university forward, or do not have the financial resources to reward (or coerce) action. It is not that they are closed out of channels of influence but they have little access to power to get things done in ways that matter to the institution and the board. One example was a trustee who spent her professional life as a second-grade teacher. She was upset that the board didn't listen to her. The problem was that the board didn't spend much time on classroom education, was in the midst of a comprehensive campaign and strategic planning process, and the university was facing financial hard times. Furthermore, other members of the board were professors and former administrators at different peer universities who had significantly more expertise about and experience in higher education.

Understanding different sources of power is helpful for three reasons beyond trustee frustration. (If the second-grade teacher had had this insight, maybe she would have had a different understanding.) First, what sources of power yield the greatest influence in the boardroom? Are most influential trustees those individuals with the deepest pockets who are able to reward or coerce action consistently and forcefully? In public boardrooms, for example, do those with the strongest ties to the governor have disproportionate influence in most or all matters, even on topics about which they know little? Do networks or rewards/coercion override expertise?

Second, is the source of influence consistent or does it vary depending on the decision or context? Do the large donors always get their way regardless of issue or do those with greatest expertise shape decisions and outcomes (or some other combination)? Are those well-connected individuals with access to ready networks or those able to provide rewards (i.e., philanthropy) influential in other situations?

Third, how consolidated is power among a subset of trustees? Is there a balance of power among trustees who are able to draw on different sources of authority? Yes, donors matter, for example, but so do those with extensive networks to help open doors for the university or individuals with deep expertise needed in the boardroom.

Understanding its source, consistency, and degree of consolidation can help boards map and understand board power dynamics.

When Power Is Overplayed

Understanding how power influences the work of the board can surface key assumptions and help boards behave differently, should they choose to do so. What follows is an example that we uncovered through the board culture profile process described in chapter 10.

At Clearlyville College, the looks were telling, as was the body language. Some members of the board did not want to hear that other trustees believed their voice and opinions mattered less than those of the trustees from the engineering industry. Those who had been talking became increasingly silent, and those who had been silent perked up. On this board, of a technology-focused college, individuals with engineering backgrounds were perceived by others, including the president, as having a disproportionate amount of influence on board matters. They tended to be the larger donors, were deeply connected to industry, and had expertise (in some areas of board work and related to the engineering programs on campus). As one person said, "When they speak, their comments become the last word on the issue, regardless of the issue." The data from our Board Culture Profile for this institution were telling but not surprising, at least to the nonengineers in the room. This 24-person board had fairly equal representation from 3 different backgrounds—engineering, academic/professional services (law and consulting), and corporate.

Almost twice as many trustees from the academic/professional services sectors reported experiencing that one subset of the board (the engineers) influenced most board decisions. As Figure 11.1 shows, other differences between these groups appeared related to issues such as the extent to which influence was tied to expertise, the ability of the board to be swayed by individuals regardless of who did the persuading, and the tendency for the board to acquiesce to a handful of individuals consistently.

This board had similar patterns related to the board's willingness to hear divergent views. Those who were not from engineering backgrounds were more likely to report that discussions were cut off for the sake of keeping

Figure 11.1. Influence: Differences by trustee background.

Percent Who Strongly Agree/Agree

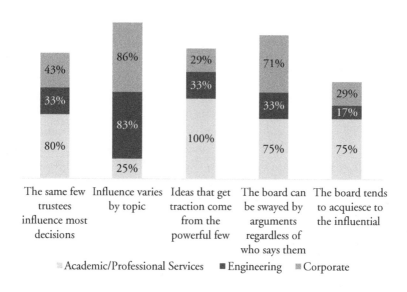

The same few trustees influence most decisions | Influence varies by topic | Ideas that get traction come from the powerful few | The board can be swayed by arguments regardless of who says them | The board tends to acquiesce to the influential

▨ Academic/Professional Services   ■ Engineering   ▨ Corporate

the agenda on time and that the board would drive for efficiency and consensus rather than consider divergent views. These patterns had entrenched themselves deeply over time and seemed to occur regardless of topic. The engineers' word was the final word on most matters.

The board had a power imbalance based upon trustee background. For this particular board, the power dynamics were not detrimental. But taken to an extreme, they could be. This board functioned well and because most of its attention addressed issues in engineering and related fields, the board contributed much. The trustees self-reported that there was high trust and candor among trustees and with the administration, and that as individuals they believed that they contributed to the work of the board. Without those positive dynamics, this board could have been facing real problems. The problem was that the board developed a habit (or rut) of listening mostly to the engineering-based trustees. They risked disengagement by a third of the board and didn't recognize when their engineering background was less important than other perspectives, such as in the audit and governance committees.

Other boards with tilted power dynamics can find themselves in trouble, and even in the headlines, for poor or dysfunctional governance. Factions emerge within the board, with one group siding with and another segment pushing against the president. Conflicts of interest can go unchecked as the overly influential can sway the board or downplay questions raised by other trustees. Or the executive committee might consistently meet before the whole board convenes, making all of the decisions and orchestrating upcoming discussions. In each of these situations, which are all too common, power dynamics are linked to poor governance.

A Tale of Two Problems

Most boards face one of two problems—either there is a power imbalance in which individuals do not have the university's best interests at heart or the board consists of high-powered individuals who do not perform well as a team. (A third option is a board of individuals of low influence, which doesn't seem like a good scenario. They still likely underperform, but for different reasons.) In any situation, boards likely end up with the mediocrity we discussed earlier in chapter 3.

Boards with a subset of overly powerful and ill-meaning trustees are often the ones that make the headlines. There frequently is no counter to their influence, regardless of the source, allowing them free reign. We frequently then see these individuals reinforce their influence (donor, network, reward, coercion) further with legitimate power. They navigate the bylaws to put themselves and their inner circle in positions of power. The more sources of influence they can tap, the greater their power can be, that they then can use for the wrong outcomes. (And in worst-case situations, they remove term limits or discount them so as to remain in positions of power.)

Boards consistently composed of high-powered individuals may also struggle with effectiveness because of conflicts in status, over directions pursued, and regarding how information is shared and used or not used (Hildreth & Anderson, 2016). Furthermore, successful individuals are more likely to stick to courses of action regardless of progress because of their past success. These individuals can be considered hedgehogs (Berlin, 1953), rather than foxes (Tetlock, 2005). Table 11.1 explains more about these individuals different characteristics in the boardroom. Hedgehogs and lions are all the more likely to dig in and stay in when they feel their reputations are on the line (Sleesman et al., 2012). Such power dynamics do not bode well for boards, but they do help explain why so many boards are merely mediocre despite the fact that they are composed of men and women of stature and prominence.

We offer two sets of recommendations depending on which type of board you have—high-powered or imbalanced power.

High-Powered Boards

Those boards comprising high-powered individuals in which the collective seems to add up to less than the sum of its parts might consider the following:

TABLE 11.1
Hedgehogs and Foxes

Hedgehogs	Foxes
Know one big thing	Know many things
Toil devotedly within one tradition	Draw from an eclectic array of traditions
Reach for formulaic solutions to ill-defined problems	Accept ambiguity and contradictions as inevitable features of life
Are characterized by hubris and self-confidence	Are self-critical and self-subversive
Are closed-minded; rarely change their minds	Utilize a dialectic or point-counterpoint style of reasoning
Are certain of their views	Are skilled at self-overhearing
Crave closure; display bristly impatience with those who "do not get it"	Listen for doubt
Dismiss dissonant data	Entertain contradictory data
Eschew tentativeness and nuance	Elevate no thought above criticism; appreciate nuance
Do not admit mistakes	Recall but do not rationalize mistakes
Rely on grand schemes and board generalizations	Are skeptical of grand schemes
Aggressively extend the reach of one big thing into new domains	Realize that a new domain is new and proceed cautiously

Source: Adapted from Tetlock (2005) as cited in Trower (2013, p. 52).

- Focus on a few tasks and priorities. These boards tend to have individuals who are accustomed to pursing their own agendas successfully. They have keen and proven abilities to determine direction on their own. But individual success doesn't translate easily into the collective tasks of governing. Minimize opportunities for individuals to pursue their own directions by focusing on a few strategic issues. Set this agenda ahead of time and communicate the importance of its focused (narrow) agenda so trustees know the objectives and will stick to them.
- Communicate effectively. It is important for these individuals to have the necessary information to govern. A challenge for these boards

is that influential individuals do not always share information with each other, says the research (Hildreth & Anderson, 2016). Formal information-sharing strategies from the administration or board leadership can be helpful.

- Be firm on meeting structure and outcomes (see chapter 6 on board agendas). Again, to keep high-powered trustees focused on the matters that matter most, ensure that the meeting agendas are clear, purposeful, and have explicit outcomes.
- Push for divergent thinking. Influential individuals likely have well-honed decision-making skills. They are successful people (hedgehogs), which means they may jump to conclusions based on incomplete information in this setting. Frame discussions using strategies that can surface different ways of thinking. Examples include assigning devil's advocate roles, structuring debates, and ending discussions with the requirement to identify counterarguments for the points made.
- Look for disconfirming evidence. Once these individuals commit to a course of action they stick to it, even if the evidence suggests a path may not be working. Use clear benchmarks and metrics and look hard for disconfirming evidence as a way to self-correct when needed.
- Let them have their status. Status is important to them individually and as a group. While acknowledging their individual accomplishments, stress their collective contributions to the board and the university or state system.

Boards With Imbalanced Power

The second type of board is that in which power is imbalanced and used ineffectively to advance board and institutional objectives. These situations can be difficult as those with the power may have consolidated it over time and are unwilling to voluntarily yield it. The following strategies may prove useful in such cases:

- Map sources of influence. Understanding the sources of power that dominate a board can help explain why the board behaves in the way it does, including who speaks and who doesn't and why some voices carry more weight.
- Name the imbalance. As the example of Clearlyville College demonstrated, discussing the data that delineated the power imbalance within the board was a meaningful experience. This board was willing to listen and to look at itself in the mirror, which isn't always the case. Despite the difficulty of confronting power directly, some boards may

nevertheless need to simply name the problem and push for change either explicitly or through back channels (such as with governor's appointment staff). Awareness is an important step, and we believe a necessary first step, toward progress.

- Work to shift the importance of different sources of influence. How might a board increase the influence associated with certain sources and concurrently begin to depreciate others. For example, if rewards or networks are the important source of potentially disruptive trustees, how might expert power be elevated in the boardroom? Or might other types of rewards be developed that shift the power base on the board?

- Use discussion methods that separate substance from source. One simple way to level the power playing field, appropriate for some board exercises, is to have all trustees respond to an important question on an index card and then shuffle the cards and redistribute them to read aloud. Because no one knows who said what, all voices carry equal weight. (Just make sure people write clearly so others can read their notecards!) Another simple way to remove the power differential is to have trustees respond to critical questions in advance of meetings through an online data-collection tool. Again, responses are anonymous, and a summary of views can be presented to the board at the meeting as a springboard for conversation.

- Focus on values. Universities are value-laden and value-based organizations. Discussing the values that are being rewarded in the board in light of what the institution values might surface a disconnect that can help temper certain sources of influence.

- Don't forget about term limits. Although not a panacea for all problems, ensuring that the board has new members can also help address a power imbalance. The issue that we have seen with this approach is that those in power simply replicate themselves in the new generation of trustees.

Conclusion: The Role of the Chair

Power dynamics in boardrooms are extremely important to how boards operate. Understanding the sources of power can be helpful. However, the ability to act upon this knowledge in beneficial ways falls to board leaders, specifically the chair (and to a lesser extent the president, who can be taking a career risk by addressing powerful trustees). Effective chairs attend not only to the issues that the board must address but also to the dynamics within the board and between the board and the president. Strong chairs who focus on group dynamics can implement strategies presented in this chapter to help move the board forward. Chairs must commit to board improvement and have a plan to follow through, which includes navigating the power dynamics present in the boardroom.

Questions for Boards

1. What are the power dynamics in your boardroom? Do you have a board of highly successful individuals or a board of imbalanced influence?
2. What are the effects of board power on how the board functions? Does power help move items forward constructively and benefit the board, or does it create difficulties? What recent examples support your responses?
3. How has the balance of power shifted over time? Has this led to better outcomes or more problems within the board?
4. How might you structure meetings to promote better board behaviors?

For Further Insight

To follow up on some of the issues raised in this chapter, we suggest:

- Chapter 3: Is Your Board Mediocre?
- Chapter 4: Individual Competencies for Collective Impact
- Chapter 6: Spending Scarce Time Wisely
- Chapter 10: The Culture of Boards: Making the Invisible Visible
- Chapter 12: The Prime Partnership Between Presidents and Board Chairs
- Chapter 13: Creating the Capacity for Trying Issues
- Chapter 15: Getting to Grips With Shared Governance

THE PRIME PARTNERSHIP
BETWEEN PRESIDENTS
AND BOARD CHAIRS

Apartnership can mean anything from an afternoon doubles tennis match to a lifelong matrimonial commitment. Partnership too describes the complexity of the relationship between president and board chair—however, without the hard and fast rules of tennis or the intricacies of marriage. This chapter examines the complex relationship between president and board chair. We argue that of the three key relationship roles—supervisor, supporter/confidant, and strategic partner—chairs and presidents tend to perform some well, but not all. To make matters more complicated, these relationships are fluid as a host of drivers, some expected, but others less so, require them to change across these three modes.

The Key Relationship

There are few relationships more important to a college, university, or state system than between the president and the board, particularly the board chair. And there are no relationships on campus more complex. "Indeed, managing this extraordinarily important and sensitive relationship [CEO-chair] over a long period of time is the greatest single challenge a nonprofit faces" (McFarlan, 1999, p. 70). We all know that boards hire presidents, evaluate them, attend meetings with them, and help them (often personally) with accomplishing professional goals, while also listening, supporting, and strategizing along with them. We know that presidents play an active role in the board, often helping to identify new trustees (particularly for private university boards, but increasingly, if indirectly, on public boards), onboard those trustees, influence and set agendas, and provide information and material necessary for boards to do their work.

This relationship is often labeled a partnership. However, a partnership can describe a wide variety of relationships, and not all president–chair relationships, like all marriages (or even doubles tennis teams) are the same. They vary depending on the individuals involved (their personalities and expectations), the institution and its needs, the external environment and its demands and dynamism, and the culture of the institution and the board and their ways of operating. However, these relationships do have some elements in common. They are complex and multidimensional; they have a power dynamic, recognized or not; and they continually evolve.

The Dimensions of a Multidimensional Relationship

Presidents and chairs have a multidimensional relationship that crosses three dimensions of work. The first dimension is accountability. For all intents and purposes, chairs and boards are the supervisors of presidents. They hold the president accountable for setting and reaching targets and goals. They influence what those goals are. Words that often describe this part of the relationship are *overseer*, *boss*, and *evaluator*.

The second dimension is the strategic partnership between president and chair. Chairs can help presidents think through direction, strategy, and leadership. Common descriptors used to capture this role are colleague, strategist, collaborator, and corroborator. Presidents can lean on chairs in ways that they cannot lean on others within the institution—to provide leadership and support.

The third dimension is the role of supporter. The job of a presidency is difficult and intense, full of contradictions that require sensemaking and trials, testing an individual's resilience. The presidency can be a lonely job and chairs can provide essential moral support. The words reflecting this function are coach, confidant, and sounding board. See Figure 12.1 for a depiction of these roles.

Figure 12.1. President-board chair roles.

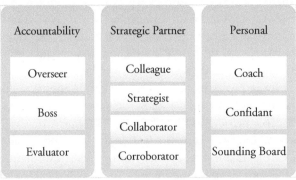

Accountability	Strategic Partner	Personal
Overseer	Colleague	Coach
	Strategist	
Boss		Confidant
	Collaborator	
Evaluator	Corroborator	Sounding Board

Although many chairs and presidents don't explicitly recognize the breadth of their collaboration, the challenge for many presidents and chairs is that they have a greater disposition toward one or two of these functions or that they are not skilled equally across them. We see presidents and chairs who think accountability first and do not pay attention to the personal dynamics of the relationship, for instance. These are the chairs who drive the oversight and accountability agendas. We see other examples in which chairs are all support and little challenge. They are there as confidants, not supervisors. In the former case, presidents may feel isolated and overwhelmed not just by the nature of the presidency but by the unrelenting focus of the chair on performance. In the latter case, chairs may not give sufficient attention to accountability. If and when something goes awry on campus, chairs who have not attended to their oversight role sufficiently may find a mess on their hands. But these examples are extreme. A more typical scenario is that two of the three aspects of the relationship are done well. Rarely are board chairs one-note wonders. Regardless of a disposition toward one or two roles, the imbalance can be challenging over the life of a presidency. It is helpful if chairs and presidents can develop the skills and knowledge to work across all three well, intentionally and able to adapt over time.

The final important relationship element that cuts across all three of aforementioned dimensions is the challenge of seeking advice. Presidents and chairs, when new, may be leery of or uncomfortable with seeking advice from the other. The literature on advice-seeking notes that people often perceive asking for help, particularly from organizational superiors, as a sign of dependency or incompetence (Westphal, 1999). This is a risk many are unwilling to take. Consider the higher education search process. After the rounds of interviews, the vetting of candidates, the negotiation of contracts, the president surely doesn't want to signal the need for assistance. The same is true of the board chair who often is selected for her or his governance wherewithal. This dynamic of the unsaid makes some collaborative work between chairs and presidents difficult.

Power Between the Players

A second key dynamic in this relationship is related to power. We explore the notion of power in the boardroom in chapter 11 but want to focus here specifically on the power dynamics between presidents and chairs.

When most people think about power related to the chair–president relationship they recognize the power that the chair holds (and can wield) over the president. The chair and the board hire, evaluate and can decide to fire the president. As Clark Kerr, the iconic president of the University of

California said, "I had left the presidency of the university as I had entered it: 'fired with enthusiasm,' my own on the way in, that of certain others on the way out" (as cited in Birnbaum, 2004a, p. 253). There clearly is a power dynamic of the board and the chair over the president.

However, there is another side to this relationship: the power that the president has over the board and the chair. As noted in chapter 11 on power and influence, French and Raven (1959) identified a set of different sources of power; some are applicable here. For instance, the president—more likely to have an academic background than most of the trustees—has expert power to leverage. The president understands higher education and the culture of the academy and has developed over time administrative and management expertise on which the board and the chair rely. Presidents also have informational power. They are the gateway to the university or state system for the board and have an understanding, including the key details, of what goes on daily that gives them another source of power. Finally, power comes with the position. The individual who is president, by nature of holding that title, gains influence at a level that others at the institution do not have.

Understanding how these sets of power matter to the relationship and to the board as a whole are important. First, as discussed in chapter 11, power matters related to the ends for which it is used. Power is neither good nor bad until it is invoked. Levering these different sources of power collaboratively to move institutional and board agendas ahead is greatly beneficial. The reverse can be said about putting them together for personal and not institutional gain. Unfortunately, we see this as well.

These sources of power can also come into conflict. When there is a power struggle between the chair and the president, regardless of which individual wins, the institution rarely does. However, depending on the aims of the president and the chair, power battles between them do occur.

We also know that the dynamics of power between presidents and chairs change over time (Shen, 2003). The longer presidents serve, the more power they accrue as they gain more knowledge and expertise and have more access to information and, in fact, control of information. Things can get especially tricky if a long-term president becomes impervious to feedback and keeps his or her board at arm's length or in the dark,

A final word about power and the president–chair dynamic. Many trustees come from corporate backgrounds and may have experience with corporate boards. Corporate chairs tend to be comparatively more influential than higher education chairs because of the structure of that position and the fact that they tend to be more knowledgeable about their industries. "Executive (chairs) are more powerful than non-executives; insiders are more powerful than outsiders; and full-timers are more powerful than part-timers"

(McNulty, Pettigrew, Jobome, & Morris, 2011, p. 98). Higher education board chairs are nonexecutive outsiders; they aren't from the organization and are from outside of the sector, and they are part-time volunteers as well. Higher education does not have full-time board chairs. (Although some retirees serving as chairs may wish this was not the case; their presidents likely do not.) These three factors create comparatively low power for higher education chairs, leaving those from corporate backgrounds often feeling they should have more direct influence than they do.

The Rules Are Rewritten

All of this said, we also know that the relationship between presidents and chairs can change on a moment's notice with the election or appointment of a new board chair or the hiring of a new president. What may be a distant relationship can quickly become intense and up close. What was once driven by facts and figures can become conversational; what had been future-focused can become about oversight and immediacy. Although presidents and chairs know this to be the case, the realities often take a while to settle in. (Eckel [2014a, 2014b] provides advice for new presidents and for chairs of new presidents in Box 12.1 and Box 12.2, which are from blog posts originally written for the AGB's website).

In one example of this fluid dynamic, the board of a private college significantly changed its ways of working and its culture under a new chair. The chair and the president moved the board from one in which meetings were highly efficient and focused, at the risk of being exclusionary, to one of greater inclusion and discussion. This required the new board chair and the president to work differently than previously. They created new types of agendas, provided different materials, and ensured that board members came prepared for more thorough discussions. This leadership change also meant that the board (because it didn't change the format of its meetings) had to agree to cover fewer issues, but in greater depth. They had to learn how to engage and discuss, not simply listen (or check their phones). They altered board operations and expectations. It also meant that the chair and the president had to change how they worked individually and together, requiring extra effort on both of their parts; however, they individually—and collectively—believed it was a worthwhile effort to lead an engaged board.

The change in presidents and chairs is particularly salient when there is a change in the gender and/or race of the individuals involved. We repeatedly have had conversations with women presidents, most who succeeded men, that gender dynamics matter, for example. As a broad generalization,

BOX 12.1.
A Letter to New Presidents

Dear New President,

First, congratulations on your appointment. I wish you much success in your presidency. Please forgive the unsolicited advice that follows; however, I (as well as your board) want to ensure you have a successful transition. While you have much on your plate, please prioritize governance and be intentional about engaging the board constructively, early, and often in your presidency.

Yes, there is much to do during your initial year, and you have an extensive range of stakeholders to meet. You also likely feel as though you have spent significant time with the board during the search process. But you and the board are in a honeymoon period. The board likes you; after all, they just hired you. And you like the board (after all, they just hired you in all their wisdom). Yet the feeling of a honeymoon can be deceiving.

If you are like the majority of new presidents, your previous interactions with a board have been limited to staffing a board committee (Eckel, 2013). Governance takes on different nuances in your current position. Here are some things to consider as you establish your presidency.

- *Spend time with the board and its leaders.* While time is your most precious resource, still make the effort to engage board members individually and as a group. Getting to know each personally will pay dividends. Get to know their talents and dispositions.
- *Learn the principles of what constitutes good governance and do an informal assessment of the board against these standards.* A strong board contributes much to an effective presidency; a weak board does just the opposite.
- *Understand your role in developing the board but know that it is a shared responsibility with board leadership.* While you are helping the board improve, keep in mind that at the same time the board will evaluate your success. The relationship between president and board is complex and one that demands a careful eye and close attention.
- *Talk to other presidents about governance.* Wisdom from experience is valuable. That said, boards are like faculties: each has its own culture and history. So rather than look for absolutes, look for lessons that might be applied to your situation.
- *Finally, think about what you need from the board both today and over the next three to five years.* The board will likely play a different role over the

course of your presidency as your leadership evolves. Plan accordingly, expect change.

I wish you all the best.

Peter Eckel

(Eckel, 2014a)

BOX 12.2.

A Letter to Board Members Upon Hiring a New President.

Dear Board Member,

Congratulations on your new president! Just like the campus, the board is also now facing a transition. This letter offers some unsolicited advice about how the board can best facilitate the transition of the new president.

- *Recognize that the new president isn't the previous president.* Obvious enough, but understand that even after an intensive search process, there is still much to learn about the new president. At the same time, the new president will likely have his or her own expectations for the board, as well as different models for what an "engaged" board is.
- *Remain focused on policy and out of management.* Trustees expecting a certain type of management style should be careful not to second guess the newly appointed president or get involved in administrative issues they think should be done differently. Remember the old adage, "noses in, fingers out."
- *Take advantage of the transition to ask questions about how well the board is working.* Boards often develop (or fall into) habits that worked well with one person, but might not work as well with a different individual. Boards can use this time of transition to focus on their own work, asking questions about how they might need to change to better support the new leader and the needs of the institution.
- *Help open doors.* If your president is like 75% of other new hires, she or he is new to campus. The board can play an important role in making new external connections by introducing and establishing the president among key external stakeholders.

Again, congratulations.

Peter Eckel

(Eckel, 2014b)

a common frustration expressed by new women presidents is that the board operates in ways most comfortable for the men, and in worst-case scenarios, like the prototypical "old boys' club." Although these new women presidents wouldn't make the point aloud, they had to work subtly to shift the way the chair and the board engaged with them. In an extreme example, one president told the story of a colleague. She said that the board chair opened his briefcase and put a bottle of scotch on the table, asking the newly hired woman president, "Where are the glasses?" It was 11:00 a.m. Monday morning. She had to politely inform him that the scotch-drinking luncheons were over. It seems that he and the former president, a male, always had a scotch when they met, regardless of the time of day. (And the chair always brought along the bottle of scotch.) Some of the disconnects related to gender and race are overt, but others are more subtle. The key point is to have a discussion about how these factors play into this essential relationship.

For many, this can be an uncomfortable discussion, but it is an important and potentially fruitful one. The dynamics change between presidents and chairs when the people change. Being sensitive to old ways of working and understanding how those habits may not allow newcomers to bring all their skills and knowledge to the challenges at hand is important.

Conclusion

This chapter intentionally does not outline the work of the president, the work of the chair, and the work they should do together. There are numerous other resources providing that guidance. Instead, it focuses on the often unstated, but widely experienced, dynamics of the relationship between chairs and presidents. The undercurrents count.

To offer a short list, though (about the work), we would advise chairs to (a) lead the board (and not the institution); (b) create highly effective and intentional meetings; (c) spend time onboarding new trustees and developing future board leaders; (d) run interference with rogue trustees; (e) provide cover to the president when needed; and (f) be thoughtful about, and effective at, three primary roles—supervisor, costrategist, and coach. We advise presidents to (a) partner with the chair to align board and institutional priorities (it's amazing how often there is a mismatch), (b) provide the needed information and resources to the chair to create and deliver effective meetings, (c) work with the senior team to effectively staff board committees, and (d) invest in developing future board leadership.

Together, chairs and presidents should (a) set board priorities and construct meeting agendas, (b) ensure the right firepower and knowledge base is onboard and leveraged appropriately, (c) set and convey expectations for trustees and for the executive and governance committees, and (d) work beyond the boardroom to advance institutional objectives such as advocating on behalf of the university. Not exhaustive lists, but sufficient to provide some direction when asked.

Questions for Boards

1. What type of engagement is easiest for the chair and president—oversight and supervision, strategic partnership, coach and confidant? What is the ideal balance among these three? How can you develop the necessary capacities to strike the right balance?
2. How is the relationship different with a new president or chair? What is said and unsaid when it comes to the dynamics? How can presidents or chairs create the space to have needed conversations?
3. How can presidents and chairs partner to move the board ahead? What are the problems to be addressed or opportunities to leverage? Through what processes will they go about leading change on the board?

For Further Insight

To follow up on some of the issues raised in this chapter, we suggest:

- Chapter 4: Individual Competencies for Collective Impact
- Chapter 6: Spending Scarce Time Wisely
- Chapter 10: The Culture of Boards: Making the Invisible Visible
- Chapter 11: The (Not So) Hidden Dynamics of Power and Influence
- Chapter 13: Creating the Capacity for Trying Issues
- Chapter 14: Strategy, Higher Education, and Boards (and Forget Planning)

CREATING THE CAPACITY
FOR TRYING ISSUES

Boards face a series of challenges over time; they may have the capacity and wherewithal to deal with some, but not necessarily all. Trying issues require boards to develop new capacities, enact new structures, and alter the focus of their work. Issues of diversity and inclusivity (and often student activism) are timely and relevant examples. Although boards have a significant leadership role to play, they are rarely poised to engage appropriately the challenging issues that most vex institutional leaders. Addressing the issues of diversity, equity, and inclusion is difficult for a host of reasons specific to these types of issues, including (a) the composition (mostly White males) of boards, (b) difficulties framing the issues for action, and (c) the complexity of the issue itself. Common governance shortcomings may also come into play, including (a) a lack of sophistication on student and faculty issues in general; (b) insufficient use of data, metrics, and dashboards; and (c) the pull of competing issues. In this chapter, we explore how to improve a board's capacity to deal with big challenges.

Equity, Diversity, and the Board

The long-simmering tensions related to race, ethnicity, inclusion, and diversity in higher education seemed to reach a boiling point nationally in 2016 and 2017. The headlines regarding protests and demands—by not only students but also faculty and staff members—at Claremont McKenna College (Pappano, 2017), Cornell College (Jaschik, 2017), the University of Missouri (Hartocollis, 2017), Yale University (Friedersdorf, 2016), and elsewhere have put such issues firmly on the agendas of boards of trustees everywhere, if they were not there already.

Then, in the summer of 2017, things heated up still more with the "Unite the Right" campaign. The University of Virginia's president, Teresa Sullivan, canceled all activities for Saturday, August 12, after tragic events unfolded in Charlottesville and hundreds of White nationalists marched and rallied on campus. Sullivan defended the right to free speech and suggested that students could stand up for their beliefs without physical confrontation (Stripling, 2017).

The headlines about violence, racism, protests, and safety have added a sense of urgency to the conversations. Although some boards have made some progress, and others have danced around the edges of such matters, most would agree that we have reached a tipping point where boards must step up and, in partnership with the president, demonstrate leadership. Diversity and equity, although extremely difficult to address constructively, are not the only trying issues that boards can ill afford to avoid. Although admittedly at various points on the thorniness spectrum, other issues may include the continued lack of success of low-income students, athletic scandals, incidents of sexual harassment and misconduct, votes of no confidence in the president, and ethical lapses by the administration. However, the issue of diversity and equity is illustrative of the type of difficult work that boards could be addressing. The contributions boards can make on seemingly intractable issues demonstrates the value that boards can add beyond their very traditional (and limited) oversight role. Using diversity and equity as a lens, this chapter examines how boards can work more intentionally to help their institutions or state systems address and stay focused on difficult and contentious issues.

Determine If the Issues Are Board-Relevant

Although boards are guided by their fiduciary duties of care, loyalty, and obedience (Association of Governing Boards of Universities and Colleges, 2015a), they may need to ask themselves when they should actively address a particularly trying issue. Using diversity and equity as an example, boards can ask themselves the following questions:

- Is this an issue about the fundamental health and performance of the institution?
- Does this issue evoke institutional core values?
- Is this issue a stated institutional priority, yet one where little notable progress has been made?
- Does it have financial or risk implications for the institution?
- Does it matter to institutional strategy?
- Is it an issue that intersects with other important topics?

Diversity, for instance, touches on all of these matters (Eckel & Trower, 2016). First, progress toward diversity has been slow for too long. The persistence and graduation rates of African American, Hispanic, and Native American students tend to lag behind their White and Asian peers. Second, most university mission statements and declarations of values include references to diversity (and, more frequently today, equity and inclusion). Third, diversity is a financial issue. The ability to recruit and retain students who are part of a changing population is in many ways about the financial well-being of the university, college, or state system. Fourth, diversity also is a strategic issue. How ready is the institution to serve diverse students and prepare them to live in an increasingly diverse world? Finally, diversity can manifest itself in areas of board work that are not immediately transparent. For example, diversity can be framed as an athletics issue. One only need reflect back on the impactful role of the football team in the diversity protests at the University of Missouri or understand that Black males, who comprise less than 4% of full-time undergraduates at public universities and colleges yet account for 55% of basketball and football players, have graduation rates that trail White student athletes, raising questions of exploitation (Harper & Harris, 2012).

Understand the Challenges of Addressing Trying Issues

Before boards act responsibly, they should first understand their own limitations in addressing the issue. Regarding diversity, boards may face challenges directly related to the issue itself as well as some indirect connections.

One direct challenge to boards advancing diversity is that they are not very diverse themselves. According to the AGB (2016), minorities comprise 24% of public university and state system board members and only 13.5% of board members of private universities. Boards often haven't adopted practices and policies of their own that advance diversity in the boardroom; these include board-level diversity statements, policies, and efforts that focus on the recruitment and retention of diverse board members and ensuring that diverse individuals prepare for and hold board leadership positions.

A second challenge is the difficulty of talking about race, ethnicity, and diversity. Without a level of comfort and familiarity by individual trustees, boards cannot hold effective discussions related to the institution and its challenges and opportunities. It's difficult to talk about race because it can feel awkward, especially when people are inexperienced. It is also a topic that can garner quick criticism and condemnation. Race has long been a hot topic in America and that continues today.

Many boards struggle when confronting issues broadly related to students and faculty. The two committees most adrift seeking purpose and focus often are the academic and student affairs committees. The issues discussed there tend to be less clear-cut or familiar than the work conducted by the audit or finance committees. Furthermore, boards may interact very little with faculty or students in meaningful and substantive ways on any topic, let alone race. The distance between boards and individuals on campus only exacerbates work related to difficult and nuanced topics. Both of these complicate board work on diversity.

Fourth, some boards fail to use relevant data and struggle to define appropriate dashboard indicators and metrics. One problem is that boards use dashboards episodically rather than regularly. Another problem is getting the right level of data. Data too deep or too narrow can lead to micromanaging and the sheer volume of data can be overwhelming or obscure what really matters. Conversely, data that are overly broad are meaningless.

Finally, higher education is a complex enterprise and boards have a significant number of serious issues to address in relatively short and structured time periods. Diversity, like other difficult issues, may be pushed off already crowded agendas. Without savvy and organized board leaders and an effective committee structure, boards struggle to get through their docket of agenda items. Diversity may be an issue addressed once or episodically, not consistently in the way that it might demand.

Develop an Approach

Although the focus of this chapter is on the issue of diversity, the steps given here might apply to other difficult board issues as well. Boards should consider the following ideas.

Ask for Numbers and Data

Boards should request meaningful data related to race, ethnicity, and socioeconomic diversity and then discuss the data and trends over the past three to five years, attempting to understand the implications of what they learn. Data inform key debates and can offer insights that move the conversation beyond anecdote and speculation. It helps ground the issues inflamed in the headlines.

Don't Simply Look at Top-Line Data

By looking at numbers more deeply, boards gain a keener insight into what is really happening. For example, in which degree programs are students of different races and ethnicities enrolling? How well are different demographics of students progressing across these various degree programs? For instance, are White students succeeding in science, technology, engineering, and math (STEM) at different rates than minority students? Do a higher percentage of minority students leave after junior year as compared to other types of students? Or do those students not return as sophomores at different rates than majority students? What about admissions and yield patterns by race, ethnicity, and socioeconomic status?

Ensure a Comprehensive Plan

In addition to the need to understand current and emerging issues, boards should ensure that the institution has an intentional plan to address each difficult issue. In any case, boards should expect a campus diversity and equity plan and ask a variety of questions: Is the plan appropriate? Does it address the right elements? Is it consistent with other institutional goals and priorities, such as those outlined in the strategic plan? Are the performance indicators sensible? How realistic is the time line? Does it clarify who is responsible for what?

Hold the President Accountable

A primary responsibility of boards is to ensure progress on institutional milestones and goals, and they do this by holding the president accountable. In turn, the board should be assured that the president is holding his or her staff team and the faculty accountable for progress, as well. By being explicit about their expectations, the board sends an important signal that it too cares about equity in a sustained and systematic manner. That said, any new goals must work in concert with other presidential priorities. Unrealistic goals and a constantly changing set of priorities do little to advance the institution or provide an effective North Star for progress.

Support the President

When the institution faces difficult and challenging issues—such as those involving race, diversity, and inclusivity—a board will also often need to counsel and support the president. Many presidents have and will come under fire for lack of perceived progress on objectives related to diversity and equity. Although some deserve the criticisms they receive, others are and have been working diligently on this agenda.

Acknowledge Complexity

Change in the academy can be difficult and seem slow, much to the frustration of some trustees. The complex and often contentious issues of diversity and inclusion are adaptive challenges, not technical problems (as discussed in chapter 8 on curiosity) with quick fixes or clear answers. In fact, treating these issues as technical problems in order to apply a tried solution may only exacerbate them.

Instead, boards must work with the president, staff, faculty, and students to examine the issues, acknowledge the complexity of views of multiple stakeholders, think critically about them, define what can be done, and take steps forward—in some cases boldly, and in others more incrementally. How boards and campus leaders frame problems is important to progress. Framing problems one way may suggest certain courses of action, as framing the challenge in a different way generates different solutions. (Chapter 8 includes a further discussion of framing the work of the board.)

Make Sure a Campus Protest Plan Is in Place

If the issue is potentially contentious or even explosive, boards should ensure that their campuses are prepared for possible protests and know their role if such protests emerge. Intentional conversations with campus leaders can help articulate a strategy and minimize any risks to people, property, and reputations.

Develop a Media Strategy Specifically for the Board

Part of the work noted previously is to ensure that the board has a clear media strategy. An effective approach includes clarifying potential questions with the board: Who speaks for the board? Who crafts the talking points? What do trustees say or not say if approached by the press?

Any communication strategy also needs to attend to social media. How are the institution and the board monitoring it? What are the means of communication that the board should pursue or try to minimize? What are the priority outlets where the board and institution should focus their attention? How agile can such media strategies be if the platforms shift, from, say, Twitter to Instagram?

Discuss Lessons Learned From Other Industries, Fields, or Sectors

Many trustees are highly effective leaders in their own industries and organizations. They may have lessons and insights to share from outside of higher education that can help campus leaders. For instance, many corporations and nonprofit organizations have made tremendous strides related to diversity and inclusion in the workplace. Others may have lessons to share from failed efforts that can also be illuminating. Boards should not shy away from serving as counselors when they have insights to share. However, as we discuss in chapter 14 on strategy, savvy boards know that not all ideas from corporate or other settings transfer smoothly into higher education. Discovering what applies well or not can only happen through a candid dialogue between the board and the administration.

Look in the Mirror

Most boards themselves have a lot of work to do regarding their own diversity. Boards should consider the ways in which issues of diversity, inclusion, voice, power, and perspective play out in their own boardrooms. It may be necessary to ask certain key questions: How diverse is the board? To what extent does it mirror the campus or larger community? What is the experience of minority board members? Do they feel their voices matter consistently? How well has the board retained minority members? Do they hold positions of board leadership?

Such conversations can be difficult to frame and hold, much like what is occurring on college campuses—yet they are essential for the board to have. People on the campus must know the board is as serious about addressing such issues within itself as it is within the institution.

Listen to Students, Faculty, and Staff

Trustees often are most comfortable in a problem-solving mode. But what may better serve their institutions is simply being able to listen to and empathize with students, faculty, and staff, withholding immediate judgment. Moving too fast to solutions without understanding the nuances of the issues on campus may provide a short-term sense of progress but create more significant challenges in the future.

Ensure Campus Policies Are Clear, Current, and Relevant

An important job of the board is to ensure that policies (e.g., for affirmative action, free speech, student rights, and diversity and inclusion) are in place and that they are clear, consistent, up-to-date, and relevant. Champlain College offers an excellent example of an institution that developed a freedom of expression statement.

With respect to process, Champlain started with why. Next, the process of creating the statement was inclusive, incorporating trustees, students, faculty, and staff. Finally, recognizing that continuous learning would be required, as the statement played out and took hold, Champlain made next steps explicit, as shown in Box 13.1.

BOX 13.1.
Champlain College Addresses Freedom of Expression

Why?

- Increased activism on college campuses nationally
- Increased dialogue/activism on our campus
- Stay ahead of the curve
- An opportunity to engage with the community to develop a shared perspective

Inclusive Process

- Board initiated work in January 2017
  - Key takeaways
    - Discussion of whether the issue requires a switch or a dial[1]
    - Recognition of inherent power dynamics
- Freedom of Expression Task Force (students, faculty, staff) convened in the spring
  - Presented drafts for feedback in classes, open forums, and an online survey

Result: Freedom of Expression Statement

Champlain College's spirit of inquiry in pursuit of knowledge supports the institution's culture of exploration with respect for diversity and a passion for an inclusive learning environment. The college holds that its community, including, but not limited to, students, faculty, staff, and invited visitors, retain the right to freely express their ideas, so long as those forms of expression do not infringe on another's freedom to do so. We believe that the commitment to engage in discomfort and controversy can promote opportunities for growth. It is not the institution's purpose or duty to protect its constituents from conflict, but rather, to create conditions for debates and discussions to flourish. (https://www.champlain.edu/about-champlain/diversity-and-inclusion/freedom-of-expression-statement)
　　Audeamus! Let us dare!

Next Steps: Continuous Learning
- Make this statement a living, breathing part of the community through dialogue among students, faculty, and staff.
- Some examples of early feedback:

(Continues)

BOX 13.1. *Continued*

- ○ Do we as a community want to explicitly state that power and identities are inextricable from the right to free expression?
- ○ The statement addressed expression. What about listening?
- ○ How do we ensure that the "other" is not the one responsible for education?
- Engage in reflective learning as we apply this statement in real time.

Note

1. The "switch–dial" discussion warrants illumination. A trustee said (paraphrasing), "We have been talking about freedom of expression as if it is a dial that you can turn to set how much freedom you want to grant. I view it as a switch; you either have freedom of expression, or you don't." In response, another trustee said that it was fine to think of freedom of expression as a switch as long as you don't have to worry about the power dynamic. He then gave an example of how he, as a person of color, felt he needed to calibrate his speech to account for the inherent power dynamics at work in majority-white settings. (personal communication, D. Laackman, January 10, 2018)

Conclusion

In sum, boards can and should become engaged in trying issues. They have important roles to play in supporting the institution as well as ensuring that it does the hard work to address such challenges. Boards that shy away from hard work may be failing in their fiduciary and leadership roles. At the same time, boards that get too far out ahead of the president, administration, and faculty also pose risk. Partnering with the president, looking in the mirror at their own behavior, and being intentional about the difficulties of addressing trying problems are essential for boards.

Diversity and equity are the focus of this chapter, but they are surrogates for other challenges. Like many others, these are long-standing issues in the academy. Boards can play a role, but that role must be intentional and nuanced. They must know when they can advance solutions and when they may be contributing to the problem.

Questions for Boards

1. What are the difficult, long-standing problems the institution has been facing?
2. What progress has it made on these trying challenges? To what extent are we satisfied with that progress?
3. What are the potential roles for the board in making progress on this issue?

4. In what ways might the board itself have contributed to the lack of progress?

5. How can the board partner effectively with the administration (and the faculty) to address trying problems?

For Further Insight

To follow up on some of the issues raised in this chapter, we suggest:

- Chapter 4: Individual Competencies for Collective Impact
- Chapter 8: Curiosity: The Boardroom's Missing Element
- Chapter 9: The "Jobs" of Committees: Of Drill Bits and Milkshakes
- Chapter 11: The (Not So) Hidden Dynamics of Power and Influence
- Chapter 14: Strategy, Higher Education, and Boards (and Forget Planning)

14

STRATEGY, HIGHER EDUCATION, AND BOARDS (AND FORGET PLANNING)

All institutions have strategic plans, yet few have boards that agree the plan is meaningful and consequential—that it has real impact on what happens or that it is an effective road map for the future, especially during turbulent times of rapid change. Strategic plans should be about intentional, institutional change. In the end, some plans become guiding documents that provide direction on paths forward, but many do not. In the minds of many trustees, the return on investment of all the effort put into strategic planning is seriously low. Although many boards encourage new approaches to planning, improving *planning* might very well be the wrong focus. In this chapter we argue that institutions and boards should focus on *strategy*, not *planning*.

A Strategy Focus

Colleges and universities spend a tremendous amount of time and efforts on their strategic plans; however, few enjoy strong consensus that they are meaningful and have real impact. Institutions form committees on campus, and often at the board level; they involve a significant number of stakeholders through numerous meetings and town halls. Plan authors spend hours crafting documents. (And, sometimes it seems, they try to figure out how to insert the word *excellence* as many times as possible.) They then participate in campus battle-based rituals wordsmithing these documents. Someone will say at one point, "A mediocre plan well executed is better than a great plan poorly executed." Yet too often strategic plans are triumphs of form over substance whose execution also falls short.

The result of all this work is a document—some long and detailed, others short and succinct. Some planning processes create guiding documents that provide a useful road map for the future, but too often many do not. Campus leaders check the planning box but are left with something of little value for driving long-term, intentional change. The return on investment of all of that effort tends to be gravely disappointing. Plans just sit on shelves, or at least on websites. Trustees wonder what all the fuss was about, why the process was so time-consuming and arduous, and why, in the end, the institution has little to show for the work. (While the president makes a good show of it all.)

Given the demands on campuses and the complexities academic leaders face, can higher education really afford to spend valuable time and talent on a project that has so little substantive impact on their future? Yes, there are latent functions of planning, such as reminding people that they are part of a larger community, but there may be other more effective and efficient ways to do this.

The solution tried and tried again on most campuses is to improve *planning* efforts to create better strategic *plans*. Involve more people; develop new metrics; hire different consultants (have leaders say earlier in the process that "this plan will not sit on the shelf"). But what happens if improving *planning* is the wrong focus? Instead, maybe institutions would be better served by focusing on the other half of the strategic planning equation—*strategy*. Boards can have a role in shifting the conversation at most institutions from one of planning to one of strategy. That is the focus of this chapter.

The Problems With Planning

The environment in which most colleges and universities find themselves demands that they develop capacities for long-term institutional change. The forces buffering higher education, that almost anyone can repeat, mean that the status quo will be insufficient for the future. Traditional ways of planning will also likely be inadequate for the future. Most plans follow a familiar template:

- They are calendar-driven (five-year plans), rather than context-driven.
- They start with what has been or where the institution is today, rather than starting with where the institution should be in the future.
- They dictate directions and priorities rather than pose questions and hypotheses about the future.
- The focus is on what the institution wants to do rather than on what the external environment might need or want; inside out, not outside in.

These approaches to planning are very much based on several implicit assumptions about the environment and the future:

- The environment is consistent, not volatile.
- The future is predictable, not uncertain.
- The future is time-dependent (that five-year focus), not challenge- or opportunity-dependent.
- The future is continuous, not disjointed.
- The environment will be familiar, not unrecognizable.

The reality is that many current assumptions won't make sense even five years hence. Institutions find themselves in volatile and uncertain environments. Challenges and opportunities do not present themselves only every five years; the future may be disrupted as well as continuous with the present, and what we understand and hold true today may be unrecognizable tomorrow.

Roger Martin (2015), former dean of the business school at the University of Toronto, has a wonderful test about the effectiveness of a plan. "If the opposite of your core strategy choices looks stupid, then every competitor is going to have more or less the exact same strategy as you" (p. 3). How many higher education strategic plans pass this test? Table 14.1 reflects the strategic goal and its opposite from two different institutions' strategic plans. They clearly don't pass Martin's test. Do the strategic choices in your institution's

TABLE 14.1
The "Martin" Test: Your Strategic Goals Versus Their Opposite Statement

Strategic Goal	*Opposite Test*
Goal: Perform High-Impact Research Strategies • Create a university ecosystem that enables the university to be an international leader in confronting the grand challenges of the twenty-first century • Foster a campus culture in which faculty, students, and staff can maximize their research productivity	Goal: Perform *Low-Impact* Research Strategies • Create a university ecosystem that enables the university to be a leader in confronting the *little* challenges of the twenty-first century • Foster a campus culture in which faculty, students, and staff can be *unproductive* researchers
Provide all students with a transformational experience	Provide all students with an educational experience that *leaves them completely the same*

Source: Based on Martin, 2015.

plan pass this test? (We provide some examples of strategic goals that pass this test from the University of Vermont College of Education and Social Services later in the chapter.)

Part of the challenge is that higher education isn't quite sure what it is supposed to be doing with its strategic plans. Some plans have operational elements such as "Increase the share of students participating in at least 2 high-impact educational practices to 90%" or "Implement a new budget model." Others include aspirational goals: "Maintain, develop, and sustain programs and activities that leverage the diversity of our students, faculty, and staff to advance our mission and education goals" or "Align our courses and curriculum with our sense of values and student learning objectives." Most plans include both types of statements. Although noble priorities, these statements are not helpful in charting an institution's future or creating a road map to get there. They are operational, not strategic.

Many plans also try to accomplish too much. They include vision statements, objectives, tactics, key performance metrics, and budgets; and they try to do this for a full 5- or 10-year window. (Can we really predict the future with that much accuracy? The iPhone is only 10 years old.) Furthermore, strategic plans attempt to merge strategy with planning with budgeting and management. The problem then in using these grand plans is that they only partially capture the reality of the institution's efforts. Much work is done off-plan. So, the plan applies when it's relevant and ignored when it is not. So much for all that time spent planning. Instead, maybe institutions should separate strategy from planning and operations by giving each its focus and seeing where that leads.

A Focus on Strategy

The central question posed in this chapter is "What would happen if colleges and universities focused on strategy rather than planning?" Strategy, as a topic, is familiar to board members with corporate backgrounds. Business schools have entire academic departments dedicated to the study of this topic. Like "leadership" or "governance," it is a searchable category for articles in *Harvard Business Review* and *McKinsey Quarterly* and one that yields thousands of articles. Yet it is a concept that has yet to take root in higher education. We talk mission (and often vision) and then plans. Strategy may be the missing bridge between these topics (see Figure 14.1).

Many institutions, including highly innovative ones, do have a strategy; it just isn't reflected in their planning documents. Pursuing adult student markets, radical plans for enrollment growth by offering new types of educational experiences (e.g., project-based learning), or launching new large-scale

Figure 14.1. Strategy: The link between mission and plans.

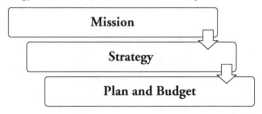

health-related research centers and initiatives all reflect strategy even if not labeled as such. Southern New Hampshire University (Kahn, 2014), Arizona State University (Marcus, 2015a), University of Maryland University College (Straumsheim, 2017), Stevens Institute of Technology (New Jersey) (Ubell, 2017), and Cabrini University (Pennsylvania) (Dimeo, 2017) are all examples of institutions with strategy. Yes, strategy does happen in higher education, but seemingly with little intentionality or rigor or across a wide group of institutions. It is not a widespread and explicit tool for institutional change.

Even though *strategy* is a topic familiar to corporate leaders, it is nevertheless one without a clear, accepted definition even in the corporate setting, and one that is even more challenging to implement effectively (thus all those *Harvard Business Review* and *McKinsey Quarterly* articles). *Strategy* has been given a variety of definitions:

- "An integrated set of actions designed to create a sustainable advantage over competitors" (Gluck, Kaufman, Walleck, McLeod, & Stuckey, 2000, p. 1)
- "An integrated set of choices that uniquely positions the firm in its industry so as to create sustainable advantage and superior value equation for a particular set of customers" (Martin, 2014, p. 83)
- "A great strategy . . . is not a dream or a lofty idea, but rather the bridge between the economics of a market, the ideas at the core of a business, and action" (Montgomery, 2012)

The final definition is particularly relevant to higher education. Universities and colleges need to articulate that bridge and do so in light of competition and the demands and opportunities of the external environment. What also is consistent across these definitions is that strategy is about choice. What strategy is not about is operations. As strategy guru Michael Porter (1996) wrote, "Operational effectiveness and strategy are both essential to superior performance . . . but they work in different ways" (pp. 61–62).

Higher education plans, often with numerous operational goals, miss the point of strategy.

Higher education seems to have a definitional problem with strategy. First, because we don't have even a notional understanding of *strategy* as compared to the corporate and health-care settings, we tend to use the term to mean many different things. Higher education leaders often use it to mean intentional or deliberate ("Let's be strategic here"). It can also denote being selective or focused ("We need to be strategic in our decision-making"). It can imply big picture or high level ("We want to focus on the strategic issues right now"). And it can simply signify an approach ("We have a strategy to align budgets with priorities").

The Utility of Strategy

What is the possible benefit to an institution and board of a focus on strategy? First, higher education does not have the resources or the support to be all things to all people. Most, if not all institutions must make choices about what to do, how to do it, and whom to serve. Second, academic institutions are deeply competitive with other institutions and nontraditional providers for, among other things, students and their tuition dollars, the attention of donors, public money, and faculty talent. Third, discussions about strategy, because they tend to be novel in higher education, might lead to a different set of ideas about long-term change and sustainability. As it is now, often the same conversations end up retreading familiar ground. A discussion starting at a different place might lead to a different set of conclusions about where an institution is heading and why it is heading there. Finally, a focus on strategy can decouple strategy from Porter's operational effectiveness. It reorganizes the work of institutional direction into discussions of where to play (strategy) and how to succeed (operations) (Lafley & Martin, 2013), rather than confusing or conflating the two. As Martin (2014) wrote, "Strategy is about placing bets" (p. 80). The better the strategy, the better the odds. Higher education is placing a lot of bets these days. Most institutions would be well served with shorter odds.

The tools of strategy may help institutions make choices and refine direction. Too many boards, faculty, and administrators are frustrated with institutional planning efforts because they provide little direction, don't frame or guide choices, and fail to chart a discernable course. (What does the objective of "transforming the learning environment" really do for an institution?)

Strategy discussions can help institutions articulate who they are and where they are going. For example, the new strategic plan at the University of Vermont's College of Education and Social Services leverages this notion of strategy. (Full disclosure: Eckel served as a consultant to the college in its efforts.) The college disaggregated its strategy from planning, or what it called "pathways." The college's strategy identifies its distinctive characteristics (who we are) and its pathways (or operational plan), setting forth how it intends to pursue its strategy across undergraduate and graduate education as well as research and scholarship, as shown in Box 14.1.

A helpful strategy framework (Lafley & Martin, 2013) utilizes three sets of questions relevant to universities and colleges (modified slightly to better fit higher education's context):

1. Where should the institution play, given its mission?
2. How will the institution succeed?
3. What institutional capacities and systems are needed?

The first two questions focus on what the institution will do and where and how it will do it; these two questions together comprise strategy and must be considered as an integrated set. Consider hotel chains. Some are geared toward business travel and others are for families on vacation. Does the firm compete for individuals traveling on company time and with company

---

BOX 14.1.
**University of Vermont College of Education and
Social Services Strategy and Vision**

We are a college of education and social services, and the impact of our work is driven by the systems orientation that we bring to the problems we address in education, human development, counseling, and social work. We strive for academic excellence in each of these areas, and we actively cultivate programmatic connections among these fields, leveraging the interconnected nature of the schools, families, and communities that we serve.

The second core component of our strategy is The Vermont Distinction, which is about the people, place, and history of Vermont.

The third strategic component driving us toward our 2022 vision is the relentless exercise of our responsibility to bring our work to life in the context of the diverse, globalized society of which we are one small part.

Our vision is to be synergistic, interdisciplinary, distinctly Vermont, diverse, global, academically vibrant, nationally recognized, and strategically resourced.

Source: https://www.uvm.edu/sites/default/files/media/CESS_Strategic_Plan.pdf

expense accounts seeking personal attention and "easy does it" or decide to try to capture the vacation dollars of families looking to get away from it all? One is about providing efficiency to a frequent traveler, the other about slowing down and smelling the flowers the business traveler just walked past (while on the phone, most likely). In the higher education equivalent, one university chooses to go after the "solid B" student. That is where they decide to play.

The how-to-succeed choices in the hotel example then focus on how well chains deliver in their respective markets. Do they offer business travelers convenient check-in, high-speed Wi-Fi, and a generous rewards program to secure repeat business; are they located near centers of business? The firms competing for family dollars might invest in quality babysitting and kids' clubs with extensive hours (two amenities not of interest to the lone business traveler). Similarly, the university in the higher education example invested in academic advising and support, career development, athletics, and facilities in its how-to-succeed efforts. Lafley and Martin's (2013) third question about the operational elements needed to effectively implement the strategy flow from the other two choices.

The University of Vermont College of Education and Social Sciences serves as another illustration. The dean and the faculty are clear in the "where to play" choices. They focus on the state of Vermont; the nexus and intersection of schools, families, and communities; and efforts that have global applications. The rest of their plan outlines its how-to-succeed priorities, which they identify as "pathways"—undergraduate education, graduate education, and research. They articulate their needed capacities and systems, the third question, in their section titled "Responsibly Resourcing a Sustainable Environment."

The process through which institutions go about answering these questions may be just as important as the answers themselves. Environments of shared governance, and the fact that much college and university strategy, particularly related to academic areas, is the culmination of a tremendous number of decisions that individual faculty and their departments make mean that strategy-setting is a collective and cumulative exercise. "Strategies are abundant in universities, as are strategists; they just cannot be found by observers who subscribe to conventional tenets of strategic management" (Mintzberg, 2007, p. 307). Process matters and unlike other organizations where strategy is set at the top, strategy in colleges and universities is a collective undertaking. (See chapter 15 for a discussion of shared governance.)

The Vermont example highlights another important element: where strategy is set. Strategy might be most valuable at the unit with salient budget authority and where competition matters most. For example, at research universities following a decentralized budget model (responsibility-centered management, or RCM), strategy may be most relevant at the school or college level. At institutions with a centralized budget model and operating in single or few markets (such as a residential undergraduate institution), strategy may be most impactful at the institutional level. The former is the case at the University of Vermont. Its RCM model and the differences among its various schools push strategy to the school level. The Larner College of Medicine will derive different answers to the "where to play" and "how to succeed" questions than the Grossman School of Business or the College of Education and Social Sciences. The responsibility for revenue and expenditures, as well as the focus of the respective colleges and schools, pushes strategy to the school level. University strategy, therefore, may be the culmination of a set of college-level strategies.

A caveat: This application of strategy from other sectors does not suggest that boards foist corporate strategy consultants onto universities to sell their wares to higher education, and particularly to the faculty. For strategy in higher education to be meaningful, the ideas most likely must be translated into the higher education community. Their utility must be demonstrated, and their impact assessed. The ideas must past the "sniff" test. (And higher education is excellent at sniffing.) Robert Birnbaum (2001), in his book on management fads in higher education, documented the frequency of and the challenges that come with seeking quick wins from ideas developed elsewhere, such as the corporate sector, and implemented in higher education. He noted that there are often "kernels of truth" (p. 246) in each management idea, from which institutions can benefit. However, he warns of the siren call of the new.

> The last [management approach] did not work, but the new one appears brilliant and failure proof. Yes, it does seem to be inconsistent with our experience of how things actually work, but the world changes. Paradigms shift. Perhaps *this* time someone has found the answer. (p. xii)

The Work of Boards

This chapter advocates for a different approach to institutional change and planning, but one that may be somewhat familiar to trustees from corporate backgrounds. Boards often struggle with their role in strategy and in strategic planning given the dynamics and expectations of shared governance. Are they involved in creating the plan or do they review plans created by the campus? This question oversimplifies the contributions that boards can make to strategy and planning efforts.

First, boards can change the focus at institutions from one that emphasizes planning to one that addresses issues of strategy. Ask institutions to review their planning documents and to discuss strategy. How much actual strategy appears in those documents? How clearly is strategy articulated? (Have institutions addressed the where-to-play and how-to-succeed questions?)

Second, trustees can share their own experiences related to strategy—both positive and negative—and reflect on how they might best share those experiences with the president, administration, and faculty leaders. What has been their experience on framing strategy? What worked well? What didn't work so well? What pitfalls did they encounter and what helped them articulate meaningful strategies for their organizations?

Third, trustees can play an active role in strategy and in planning. The three-part framework of trustee work presented in chapter 1—oversight, stewardship/problem-solving, and strategy/problem-finding—can be a useful framework for the board's role in strategy. Boards have important contributions to make across all three domains when it comes to strategy and planning.

Regarding oversight, Richard Chait (2009) outlined key questions for boards related to this role:

- Are the plans consistent?
- Are the tactics plausible?
- Are the risks reasonable?
- Are the milestones feasible?
- Are the metrics sensible?

These are oversight questions. They look retrospectively at plans and their components. Ask institutional leaders to be accountable for progress as well as the components of plans.

Boards also can play a stewardship or problem-solving role related to strategy and planning. They can ask the following questions:

- Is the planning/strategy process sound? Does it involve the right amount of people? Does it tap appropriate bodies of shared governance?
- Is the engagement appropriate? Does it adhere to institutional (faculty) expectations for involvement and thoroughness?
- Does the plan focus on strategy (where to play and how to win) as well as operations?
- What assumptions does the plan reflect about the institution, its competitors, the future of higher education, and the environment? Are these assumptions solid?

The final set of questions boards can ask of the strategy and planning work focuses on problem-finding or strategy itself.

- What do we believe about our students and prospective students? How will they be similar or different in the future?
- What are our competitive advantages and how can they be further leveraged?
- How is higher education evolving as a sector? What does this mean for whom we serve? How we educate them? And how will we pay for it? (Same with research.)
- What do we believe about how competition is changing? How might our current competitors act differently? What new competitors might we anticipate? How will they compete?
- What are the unforeseen challenges or opportunities that we have not explored?

Finally, boards need to be understanding and supportive of the fact that strategy is indeed a bet, with no guaranteed outcomes (Martin, 2014). They need to ask good questions but be encouraging of the directions and bets the administration and the faculty are willing to place.

Conclusion

Most universities and colleges are facing challenges requiring them to think, change, reflect, and adapt much more quickly than ever before. Therefore, traditional strategic planning efforts that take a long time and seek input from numerous stakeholder groups through complex committee structures and shared governance processes better suited to a bygone era are putting additional stressors on decision-makers. This chapter argues that adopting a different approach to strategic thinking and strategy might be advantageous. Trustees, many of whom have experience with strategy in their professional settings, can help shift the traditional planning conversation in higher education. Too much time and attention has been given to planning without considering strategy. Strategy offers numerous tools from which higher education might benefit by appropriately leveraging and translating in ways that fit the contours and expectations of higher education. That said, as Birnbaum (2001) cautioned:

Good academic management is not the same as good business management, and uncritical acceptance of management innovations and fads invented to meet the needs of government, business or the military is more likely to harm than benefit colleges and universities. On the other hand, thinking about how elements of fads [or outside management frameworks] might provide new insights into improving institutional management can be very valuable. (p. 240)

Questions for Boards

1. What is the return on investment of the institution's strategic planning effort? How do its current efforts matter?
2. To what extent are our strategy efforts aligned with the realities of the external environment (e.g., disjointed, unpredictable, and problem- or opportunity-driven)?
3. Have current efforts confused strategy with planning? And with what effects?
4. What are the choices we have made regarding where to play and how to succeed? How clearly articulated are those questions?
5. What is the role of the board in campus strategy? What are our roles of oversight? Stewardship?
6. How can we lend insight into institutional strategy? What relevant experiences might we translate into higher education?

For Further Insight

To follow up on some of the issues raised in this chapter, we suggest:

- Chapter 6: Spending Scarce Time Wisely
- Chapter 8: Curiosity: The Boardroom's Missing Element
- Chapter 9: The "Jobs" of Committees: Of Drill Bits and Milkshakes
- Chapter 13: Creating the Capacity for Trying Issues

GETTING TO GRIPS WITH
SHARED GOVERNANCE

Trustees new to serving on the boards of colleges and universities some-times feel as though they've entered an alien world, with Byzantine structures, outdated business models, and strange practices like life-time employment for tenured faculty. And long-serving trustees wonder why they are still surprised and confused by all of this. Among the oddest features of academia is shared governance. Why would those with legal authority, and who are ultimately accountable for the enterprise, delegate responsibility in diffuse fashion to employees? This chapter addresses that question.

Why Shared Governance

Serving on a college or university board is at once familiar (because trus-tees fondly recall their college years and they get to talk about finance) and strange (because they now have to navigate a complex milieu of which they were unaware as students). This is where shared governance—a topic that seemingly flummoxes many boards—resides. Trustees wonder what shared governance is, how it works, and why it functions like it does. Part of the challenge for boards regarding shared governance is that many trustees value results over process and answers over questions. Most boards believe they have been effective when they come up with good answers and vote on things. (We argue in chapters 6 and 8 that effective boards also ask effective questions.) The difficulty with shared governance for most boards is that it rarely yields answers, but instead continually surfaces questions, and sometimes problems. (Note that the chapter title is getting to "grips," not "gripes," with shared governance. That addition of the letter *e* means a lot. The fact that readers skimming quickly may have missed that difference also says a lot.)

There are six principles that boards should keep in mind when getting to grips with shared governance. These principles are intended to help trustees understand the fundamental nature of shared governance, its dynamics, and its contributions to campus. From this understanding, trustees can determine how to engage within their own culture and context. Our focus is on *why* things happen rather than *what* to do. Finally, a word about language. We use *shared governance* in this chapter, but other language to describe similar phenomena includes *faculty* or *campus governance*. Technical distinctions exist, but they are not central to our discussion. We also use the term *senate* to mean the most typical formal shared governance body.

Principle 1: Shared Governance Is a Way of Life in the Academy

Most colleges and universities, and even state systems, have shared governance bodies. Mostly called faculty senates, these entities and the rules surrounding their operation are codified in policy handbooks. The scope of their work varies from one campus to another, but for the most part, it centers on matters of academic and institutional policy.

Their very existence and their level of authority tend not to have parallels in the corporate settings from which most trustees come (Association of Governing Boards of Universities and Colleges, 2016). There are some counterparts in hospitals, but, in the main, these bodies and their approaches to organizational decision-making are atypical outside higher education. Thus, most individual trustees have little experience and familiarity functioning within such decision-making systems.

Although boards hold the ultimate legal authority for their institutions, shared governance blurs this line of rights. Administrators learn early in their tenures about the importance and power of shared governance. As former university president Donald Walker (1979) noted, "If there is an issue at hand that the faculty cares deeply about, and you can't convince them you certainly can't bulldoze them" (p. 10). More than one president and board have found out the hard way that they must work with, not run over, the faculty.

Shared governance seems to play by its own rules, and it does because those rules fall outside administrative lines of authority. Although trustees draw their authority from their position atop the institution's hierarchy and delegate that authority to presidents and administrators, shared governance draws its authority from the professional standing and role of faculty. Universities and colleges, from an operational perspective, have dual sources of authority—administrative and academic (Mintzberg, 1983). Bureaucratic authority is tied to the legal status of the board, which is delegated to senior administrators. The second source of authority—professional—originates from the knowledge, expertise, and specialization required to perform the core functions of the institution (i.e., teaching and research). The result: Authority is not consolidated predominantly in the hands of the organization's positional leaders like in corporations, the military, or other organizations. Instead, it is diffused, more like law and consulting firms.

It is common within colleges and universities to say that authority is shared (and thus the label *shared governance*), but the reality is that two types of authority exist. Depending on the topic and the context (e.g., budgeting and planning), administrative authority can be the stronger source. However, professional authority is dominant in decisions about faculty hiring, curricular offerings, and the research that is pursued. The clash occurs when both types of authority stake claims on the issue at hand. For example, is closing academic programs an administrative responsibility tied to budgets, strategy, and direction, or is it curricular in nature related to what is taught and to whom? The answer is yes.

Principle 2: Shared Governance Is Not Only a Structure; It's an Idea and a Value

Although shared governance has been described as a long-standing "institutional value" of campus constituents (Minor, 2004, p. 346), most boards and administrators, and even some faculty members, think of shared governance in structural terms. For instance, the faculty senate or academic council is shared governance. Although the focus on structure is accurate to an extent, the bodies of shared governance are really the manifestations of the *idea* of shared governance. Therefore, criticisms of governance and efforts to "improve it" that focus on the structural aspects of governance and fail to recognize its "soft" cultural aspects (Birnbaum, 2004b) may miss the mark and exacerbate problems. Shared governance is more than the bodies, reporting lines, and policy documents of campus decision-making. It is a set of social connections and interactions that help institutions function collectively, despite their loose coupling (Birnbaum, 1988; Weick, 1976). Loose coupling is evident when elements in a system—like academe—affect each other "suddenly (rather than continuously), occasionally (rather than constantly), negligibly (rather than significantly), indirectly (rather than directly), and eventually (rather than immediately)" (Weick, 1982, p. 380).

The long-standing criticism of shared governance is its inability to make decisions quickly and effectively. Today, there are even more passionate criticisms: "In today's digital world, it is hard to exaggerate the importance of having educational institutions . . . benefit from the ability to make decisions promptly, and then to change course if need be. Nimbleness is a real virtue"

(Bowen & Tobin, 2015, p. 185). However, because shared governance is an idea as much as a structure, its function is more than to make decisions. It helps create and maintain a sense of community through the embodiment of values, including faculty expertise and prerogative, inclusivity, debate, and thorough examination of issues.

> Most people in a college are most of the time less concerned with the content of a decision than they are with eliciting an acknowledgment of their importance within the community. We believe that some substantial elements of the governance of universities can be better understood in terms of such a hypothesis than in terms of an assumption that governance is primarily concerned with the outcomes of decisions. (Cohen & March, 1986, p. 121)

Efforts to improve shared governance—typically about decision-making efficiency—may actually run counter to the very idea of shared governance. "The greatest danger to higher education may be not that decisions are made too slowly because of the drag of consultation, but that they are made too swiftly and without regard for institutional core values" (Birnbaum, 2004b, p. 6). Although the focus on decision-making is an attempt to create better decisions, considering shared governance as an idea may create better universities.

Principle 3: Shared Governance Is Inconsistent Across Institutions and Over Time

Because shared governance is more than an organizational structure, it varies from institution to institution, and even within a single institution, and it is continually changing and morphing (and not always for the better).

Shared governance is not uniform in higher education. What is considered part of or essential to shared governance at one institution may not be part of the construct at another institution. Institutional culture and history shape what is considered as legitimate faculty prerogative. For example, at one institution an ad hoc task force of faculty, administrators, and trustees may be considered legitimate and seen as doing good work. But at a similar institution such an effort sets off alarm bells among the faculty of administrative and board overreach even if they are addressing the same issue through a comparable structure. Therefore, boards should tread carefully regarding generic advice about shared governance or national reports on shared governance (and what boards should do), especially when they don't acknowledge institutional differences or define what they mean by *shared governance*, not just in decision-making structures but in institutional cultural terms.

Shared governance within institutions is also fluid. Because it is shaped so much by campus understandings and values, as well as by its participants and their agendas, it is continually changing. The focus and priorities, as well as the players, shift. Therefore, a topic that was important to yesterday's faculty body may no longer be relevant to today's, and an issue that was clearly the domain of administrators in the past can become owned by the faculty today. Understanding the rules of the game today does not mean those same rules will be in place in the future. Governance is organic. "The best forms of governance are those that evolve because they are most fit for a specific end" (Birnbaum, 2004b, p. 24). Shared governance is a moving target, or a movable feast—choose your metaphor.

Principle 4: Shared Governance Has Latent Purposes

The work and impact of shared governance is broad and deep. Its bodies, such as the campus senate, do things that most expect shared governance to do, such as make decisions, but these bodies also do things that are unexpected and therefore may go unnoticed—the latent functions of senates (Birnbaum, 1989, p. 428). Wise boards are aware of and appreciate the latent functions of senates and other shared governance structures, manifested in a variety of ways:

- Sign of faculty authority. Senates and other shared governance bodies "are a symbol of administrative acceptance of the ideas of faculty participation in governance" (Birnbaum, 1989, p. 429). Furthermore, senates are symbols of cooperation between the faculty and the administration. Finally, senates certify the status of faculty in the organization by acknowledging their right to participate in governance. Senates and shared governance bodies are important not because of what they do, but because they exist and what they mean to those involved.
- Commitment to academic issues. In the midst of national and institutional conversations about higher education's broken business model, Moody's outlook reports, and disruptive innovation, senates serve as reminders of academic and faculty priorities. The fact that they exist and the topics they address signal to the institution and other stakeholders that academics and their concerns matter. Senates are an expression of academic relevance and importance and that universities are different from other types of organizations.
- Opportunities for certain faculty to gain and convey status. Status in university communities is earned and expressed in many ways, through what happens in the classroom (outstanding teaching) or in the lab (research productivity and external funding). Another way

is through participating in governance. For some faculty, this too provides a validation of significance.

- Limiting the damage to institutions that can accrue from speed. Because senates are inefficient as decision-making bodies, they can serve as an institutional "deep freeze." It is not uncommon for a senate committee to take so long to study an issue that it eventually is no longer of pressing interest. If presidents don't know what to do, creating a committee can buy time. Issues "may be referred to the senate with the justifiable expectation that they will absorb a significant amount of energy and then will not be heard of again" (Birnbaum, 1989, p. 432). Senates also offer faculty an institutionally recognized forum to vent their frustrations. Thus, time spent griping on the senate floor is not time spent disrupting more vulnerable institutional activities where faculty can do real damage (e.g., in their home departments or directly with students).

- Shared governance can function as a scapegoat. The senate can be, and often is, blamed for many institutional shortcomings. It is much easier for a president to explain that an issue is under investigation by the senate than to tell trustees that the issue the board has suggested is not really a priority.

- Helping reveal what issues are of real importance. "Not every item that is proposed for the senate agenda actually gets on it, and not every item that gets on it is attended to" (Birnbaum, 1989, p. 433). Therefore, shared governance becomes a sorting and prioritizing mechanism that "relieves the administration of the responsibility for dealing with every problem" (p. 434).

- Administrative training ground. Election to a senate or similar body may be evidence that a particular person has the trust of peers to work on institutionally important issues. Furthermore, through shared governance work, individuals gain experience working with administrators and they become more knowledgeable about how administrators approach problems, allowing faculty to test the waters of administration before taking the plunge.

In sum, the senate and other shared governance bodies can be institutionally effective even if they are perceived to be inefficient at making decisions. They contribute in numerous (latent) ways beyond the scope of their decision-making responsibilities. As Birnbaum (1989) reminds us, the senate is "a place where speeches can be made, power can be displayed, nits can be picked, and the intricacies of *Robert's Rules of Order* can be explored in infinite depth" (p. 437). These and the other listed activities may serve important functions on campus beyond rendering decisions.

Principle 5: Shared Governance Requires Intentional Leadership by Faculty

Good senates are led by effective leaders—faculty who understand the challenges facing the institution and who are respected by their peers. Such leaders identify worthwhile issues and frame reasonable work; they also distinguish important from irrelevant issues, understand how the different pieces fit together, and communicate effectively with faculty peers and the administration (Eckel, 2009).

Effective faculty leaders understand their colleagues. They can articulate constructively the concerns and challenges their peers are facing, often in ways that the individuals cannot. They have a finger on the pulse of the institution and listen well. They are credible.

Additionally, these individuals develop the skill to be translators between different parts of the institution; they can explain the experiences and worries of faculty to administrators and the board, and they can explain administrative and trustee perspectives to their academic peers. They can build bridges between different stakeholders and facilitate effective two-way communication.

Finally, effective senate leaders must have the managerial skills to build effective meeting agendas and facilitate meaningful discussions at those meetings. Faculty leaders must have the patience, foresight, and talents to be effective in the work of governing. (They share much in common with effective board chairs.)

Finding and developing faculty to lead in this capacity can be a challenge. Some individuals are natural leaders. And there is very little, if any, formal training for would-be faculty leaders. Instead, most faculty leaders learn in the trenches. Some learn effective approaches, but not all. More intentionality paid to developing faculty leaders makes good sense because of the complexity, ambiguity, and nuances of the problems we face in higher education and the fact that faculty work autonomously. The challenge is that all cylinders must be firing and firing consistently and repeatedly for shared governance to be an effective decision-making body.

Principle 6: Effective Presidents Learn How to Work With and Appreciate Shared Governance

Boards want to support their presidents. They seek to ensure that the individuals they hire, counsel, and hold accountable are effective in their positions. Key to the success of presidents is their ability to work well with shared governance bodies. These relationships can be challenging and difficult and they can be rewarding and constructive. Research suggests that the dynamics between faculty and presidents evolve over time (Birnbaum, 1992). Most presidents begin with good will and positive relationships with faculty. Some presidents maintain constructive relationships with faculty, but others lose support over time. Failed presidents are those who become distant and isolated from the faculty, self-centered and closed to influence. In contrast, the key to long-term success is faculty perception that presidents are not only technically competent but also demonstrably concerned with faculty and open to their influence. Successful presidents

> were seen as honoring and working within established governance structures, accepting faculty participation in decision-making, and being concerned for process. They also had a strong sense of values that were consistent with the purposes and missions of the institution but at the same time transcended them. (Birnbaum, 1992, p. 5)

Getting a Firm Grip

What does this all mean for boards? The relationship between boards and faculty governance, for the most part, is distant and episodic. Boards and faculty may be in the same room only infrequently and for short amounts of time, and each time they are together, the agenda may be tightly scripted. Furthermore, the participants might differ each time. The interactions can seem like a cross-cultural excursion rather than a gathering of two members from the same tribe.

Boards are well served to keep the following in mind regarding shared governance:

- Shared governance is an essential part of the higher education decision-making process and culture. Shared governance is a foreign notion to most trustees, but just because it is different doesn't mean it is folly.
- Shared governance makes important organizational contributions beyond rendering decisions. It signals and symbolizes much—participation, faculty voice, and the priority of academic issues.
- The fact that shared governance is inefficient may be a blessing in disguise precisely because it slows things down. And there are ways, with concerted effort on the part of administrators and faculty leaders, that shared governance mechanisms and bodies can render effective decisions on even the most challenging issues.

- Suggesting—or worse, mandating—changes to "improve decision-making" may actually do more harm than good. The goal of shared governance should be to build better institutions, not to develop more efficient decision-making processes.
- The work of shared governance is just that—work. It takes intentionality and time on behalf of administrative and faculty leaders to work constructively through shared governance mechanisms.
- Maintaining support from the faculty is important to the continued success of a president—one of the board's primary charges.
- The faculty and those who participate in formal shared governance bodies, such as the senate, are a diverse group. There are few times in which "the faculty" are unanimous on anything. Therefore, broader engagement can lead to alternative paths forward, if and when one trail seems to be a dead end or cul-de-sac.

None of this discussion is intended to be apologetic for shared governance. On many campuses it falls short of expectations and is an impediment to institutional progress. But on other campuses it is an essential element of institutional high performance. Regardless of the impact, boards are well served to know more about this steadfast characteristic of academic life.

They Are Us; We Are Them

Faculty governance actually shares a tremendous amount in common with board governance. Looking across the aisle may be a look in the mirror. Richard Chait (2000) noted that "simply stated: Trustees and professors act more alike than they often realize, and the very tendencies that they share contribute greatly to the exasperation that each group feels toward the other" (p. 2). Chait noted several commonalties between faculty and trustees and pointed out that both sides likely see certain behaviors in the other, but not in themselves:

- Deadwood: "Each side overestimates, probably by a wide margin, the number of sloths on the other's rolls" (p. 9). And neither side does much about its own underperforming members.
- Organizational conservatism: "Trustees and faculty members contend that the other's governance system is ineffective or ill-suits the current challenges to higher education" (p. 10). Faculty criticize board micromanagement and trustees criticize cumbersome shared governance processes. Both groups love their committees. Furthermore, neither boards nor faculty senates have done much to

change how they function. "Each side tends to attribute the other's conservativism to an unwarranted and intrinsic fear of change, but then justifies its own adherence to the status quo as rationally based" (p. 10).

- Unsolicited advice: "Trustees hear no shortage of recommendations from professors about how to run every aspect of the institution" (p. 10). In turn, "board members urge that colleges adopt management techniques incubated in industry, but they show little concern for the problems of . . . transferring ideas wholesale from one organizational culture to quite a different one" (p. 10).

- Inconsistency: Both "trustees and faculty members often seem better equipped to prescribe than to enact" (p. 11). Both groups are keen to offer recommendations to the other but don't seem to act on their own advice. Trustees recommend, for instance, performance measures for institutions but don't develop their own indicators. Faculty want openness but do much of their committee deliberations away from external eyes.

One lesson we can draw from these parallels is that the more engagement between boards and faculty, the more likely they will see themselves in the other and find ways to mutually move forward together. To be able to do this well, both sides need to understand the other, how they work, and their constraints and shortcomings.

Conclusion

Shared governance—with the right relationships between the administration and board—does work and can add value, both in helping to render decisions and take action and for its latent functions. It can even play constructive roles as institutions make some of their most challenging decisions, like closing academic programs (Eckel, 2009). For such an institutional decision, shared governance can provide (a) the platform from which administrators can gain a commitment to close programs, (b) the vehicle through which different stakeholders and interest groups can come together in legitimate ways to accomplish high-stakes tasks, and (c) a mechanism that informs decisions that both shape outcomes and help correct potential errors. Shared governance is important to both administrative and institutional success. It requires intentional effort on the part of university leaders, but shared governance matters.

In many ways the characteristics and contributions of shared governance are appearing in corporate America. *Harvard Business Review,* the exemplar of contemporary management thought, is rife with articles that promote flat hierarchies, shared decision-making, devolved or employee-driven strategy, knowledge workers and the creative class, and self-managed teams. "Progressive management thinkers have been talking about worker empowerment for decades" (Martin, 2010, p. 71). Higher education has been using it for centuries. In today's world of expected revolution and change, universities continue to be extremely resilient.

Questions for Boards

1. What does the board really know about shared governance on campus?
2. What is the president's view on the status of shared governance on campus?
3. What are examples of when shared governance worked well and examples of when it didn't? What may account for the difference? What are the lessons learned?
4. How can the board appreciate the different types of contributions that shared governance makes, both explicit and latent to the institution?

For Further Insight

To follow up on some of the issues raised in this chapter, we suggest:

- Chapter 2: The "Damned If You Do, Damned If You Don't" Dynamics of Governing
- Chapter 8: Curiosity: The Boardroom's Missing Element
- Chapter 11: The (Not So) Hidden Dynamics of Power and Influence
- Chapter 12: The Prime Partnership Between Presidents and Board Chairs

---

16

GOVERNING CIRCA 1749

Individuals reading this book are looking for answers to their governance questions. In seeking such answers that will help trustees address today's problems and prepare for tomorrow's challenges, people tend to look ahead. Asking how can we get ahead of the curve? Rarely do people look to the past. (Although history is said to repeat itself.) This chapter does just that, and it looks very far back to glean insights for today's boards. The University of Pennsylvania's (Penn's) board first started meeting in 1749 and kept a set of minutes. Those handwritten minutes contain insights that are highly relevant today, even if today's minutes are captured electronically and presented on web portals and e-board books.

Viewing Today From Yesterday

As college and university boards seek strategies for more effective governance, they look to many places—other university boards, hospitals and nonprofit organizations, and corporate boards. However, looking to history, interestingly enough, can also prove fruitful to find solutions to today's challenges.

Then called the Academy of Philadelphia, Penn's board first started meeting in 1749. And like all good boards, it kept a set of minutes (University of Pennsylvania, 1749–1768). Those handwritten minutes of Penn's earliest board meetings are available through the university's archive. They contain fascinating elements, such as founder Benjamin Franklin's signature (which is pretty cool), and show that Franklin was elected president, with responsibilities paralleling today's board chair. However, the earliest Penn board minutes can and do reveal much more. They provide lessons, culled here from board minutes from November 1749 through March 1752, that even 267 years later are surprisingly instructive for today's trustees. The following quotations come directly from the handwritten minutes. As a reminder, the events on which these lessons are drawn occurred a full 16 years *before* the establishment of our nation. They offer common sense on university governance before Thomas Paine wrote (a very different) *Common Sense*, about a different type of governance.

Elect Savvy Board Leaders, but for Fixed Terms

Although not exactly the equivalent of Franklin, today's boards do have extremely talented individuals. Institutions should seek accomplished individuals to serve on their boards. They may come from their alumni ranks, but they need not. Franklin's board had no alumni, as you might have guessed. Boards need outstanding individuals, if they can and are willing to make the commitment of time necessary, to serve as board leaders. Franklin, just such a person and Penn's founder, played a role similar to board chair once the head of the academy was hired. Franklin—statesman, educator, scientist, inventor (and first postmaster)—had the skill set, curiosity, and intellect to make any board chair envious. These skills and the others that he developed through his different roles might serve as models for today's chairs.

Chairs need to master the craft of diplomacy within the board, between the board and the president, and with external stakeholders. They should be committed to the educational ideas of the institution they serve. They should be innovative and clever, and they often forge pathways where none previously existed. They should ask questions that push the boundaries of what the board takes for granted. And, for the postmaster in us all, they should be organized to run meetings effectively. (No one wants their board books "lost in the mail" or board meetings to lose sight of their agendas and objectives.)

The academy's constitution set forth the role of the chair, explaining

> whose particular duty it shall be, when present, to regulate their Debates, and state the proper Questions arising from them, and to order Notices to be given, of the times and places of their special conventions. And the like election shall be annually made, at their first meeting after the expiration of each year. (University of Pennsylvania, 1749–1768)

The creators of this colonial board were shrewd in many ways. First, they created term limits for the chair, although they could be renewed (as they were for Franklin). Maybe it was the roots of early American democracy, but this nascent board decided early on that power was to be limited. It is not unheard of for chairs, particularly at those institutions in the news for all of the wrong reasons, to become power-hungry (something we discuss in chapter 11). The limits of power may serve boards well as it has our nation. Moving on can be difficult for many individuals who become emotionally attached to their institutions. Often, they believe there is no one who can replace them. That might be true, at least in the short term, but today's boards have many more accomplished citizens than Franklin's colonial board, and they implemented term limits.

Second, the meetings of Franklin's board were expected to be *debates*. We believe that today's boards should have that same expectation: the ability to debate issues from informed positions. It takes commitment by board members to build necessary knowledge and effective leaders to effectively frame issues that will benefit from debate. As Peter Drucker (1990) wrote about boards 200-plus years later, "It is to the benefit of an institution to have a strong board. . . . You [the president] depend on the board, and therefore you can be more effective with a strong board, a committed board, an energetic board, than with a rubber stamp. The rubber stamp will, in the end, not stamp at all when you most need it" (p. 178). Clearly this colonial board had no expectation for being a "rubber stamp" board. (That is even before rubber was used to make stamps—a wax-seal board, maybe? Doesn't quite have the same ring to it.)

Finally, these early trustees recognized that good chairs not only manage meetings—*regulate debates* in their parlance—but also frame the questions for the board to address. Chairs not only steer; they also probe. Helping boards ask questions remains an ongoing challenge for many boards. Frequently boards are good at making statements and offering wisdom and answers, but they may not ask enough well-informed and thoughtful questions. (See chapter 8, on curiosity, for more.)

Encourage Philanthropy and Lead by Example

This colonial college, like most others, struggled financially in its infancy. Many universities and colleges today face similar financial challenges. Trustees then, as now, were encouraged to use their wealth as well as their wisdom to advance the early college's mission. The bylaws encouraged board members to

> furnish them [the students] with Books of general use, that which might be too expensive for each Scholar [student], Maps, Draughts, and other things generally necessary for the improvement of the youth, and to bear the incumbent charges that will unavoidably attend this undertaking, especially in the beginning.

The minutes continue:

> The Donations of all Persons inclined to encourage it are to be cheerfully and thankfully accepted.

Today, as then, donations should be "cheerfully and thankfully accepted." Not to confuse governance with philanthropy, the financial support provided by the trustees for their institution is nevertheless important. Although most universities have moved beyond the need for donated maps, books, and draughts (what today we call checkers), they still need resources, particularly for low-income students.

As seen in the minutes from April 1751, philanthropy continued to play an important part of the work of the board.

> Ordered that the thanks of the trustees be given by the president [Franklin] to the Reverend Mr. Peters for his excellent sermon preached in the Academy Hall . . . at the opening of the Academy.

Those same minutes continued:

> Ordered that the *hearty* thanks of the trustees be given to Mr. Lawrence for his generous donation of 100 pounds for the Academy. (emphasis added)

Whereas the keynote speaker at the very opening of the academy was thanked ("Nice job, Reverend"), the person donating cash was thanked heartily. It seems that the 100 pounds was even more appreciated than the Reverend Peter's words of wisdom given the reported board enthusiasm. Even then, no money, no mission.

Manage Risk

Not all philanthropy is desirable, even for a college starting before this nation was built. In December 1750, at the board's second meeting, Franklin delivered a letter to his fellow trustees that offered land from a benefactor on which to build a new building for the academy. As the minutes noted, the board directed Franklin to say

> that the trustees had a most grateful sense of his regard to the Academy, but . . . they could only return him their sincere thanks for his kind and generous offer.

Their minutes mention that their current building

> was in all respects better suited to their present circumstances.

A lesson from this early experience is to be gracious to potential donors even if you turn down their generosity. Consider the gift and all that it brings, both positive and negative. It is likely that this board didn't use language such as "upside and downside risk," but nevertheless that is the debate they seemed to have. Today's boards would be well advised to do the same.

Understand That the Engagement of Outstanding Individuals Is Difficult to Sustain

Like many of today's boards, encouraging trustees, who tend to be busy and accomplished individuals, to participate consistently in board meetings is difficult, and their lack of attendance can be frustrating. People like Franklin, and others involved with this early board, were busy laying the foundation for what was to become the United States of America (a pretty good reason for missing board meetings now and again). They, too, struggled with engagement. Nevertheless, this early board tried a couple of different approaches to improve attendance, which we're not sure we recommend.

First, they tried a bit of public shaming. The early minutes note not only which trustees were in attendance, but also listed those who were not. We're not sure who Thomas Hopkinson was or what he was doing, but he got called out time and again for his absences. Although we don't suggest public shaming of trustees, boards do need to try different tactics to improve engagement.

That said, what the academy's board tried next might not be suitable today, but it is interesting in how this early board stepped up pressure to encourage participation. In April 1752, it was

> Agreed by the Trustees present to pay a Fine of One Shilling if absent at any meeting, unless such Excuse be given as the Majority shall judge reasonable. The Money to be applied towards buying books, paper for the scholars [students] in the Charity School.

There was a financial penalty for missing board meetings, but the fine was to go toward a scholarship fund. In many ways, it was a precursor to a trustee scholarship fund. But instead of incentivizing participation, it was punitive.

Beyond the monetary point, this approach may importantly highlight tensions within the board. As likely happens in today's boardrooms, those who voted on this policy of fines were the ones present at the meeting, looking for ways to twist the arms of those who were absent. This pattern suggests a similar frustration for today's trustees who constantly participate and become put off by colleagues who rarely show up. Many hardworking trustees then and now are bothered by carrying the load of those who repeatedly miss meetings. And in this early board, they could not join by teleconference or video-chat. You were there in person or you were not.

Alas, even these escalating tactics didn't work. The minutes from a board meeting in March 1753 contain but a single line:

> But few of the Trustees met, and no business was done.

Trustees continue to wrestle with ensuring engagement. However, relying on busy and accomplished individuals, now as the Penn board did then, was an ongoing and continuous challenge. It's just a good thing that the nation isn't preparing for revolutionary wars now as it might be even more difficult to recruit well-qualified individuals to serve as trustees and keep them sufficiently engaged.

Use Committees Wisely

This colonial board developed a committee structure. Interestingly, the earliest committees were what we would now recognize as buildings and grounds or facilities committees, advancement (someone had to offer "sincere thanks for kind and generous offers"), finance and audit, and academic and student affairs (what they called the committee on the "Rules for the Regulation of several schools"). The first board committee (what might be grounds or facilities) was created for

> Some of the Gentlemen appointed to meet with Workmen concerning the alterations necessary to be made in the New Building.

They later created other committees and task forces for increasingly strategic discussions. For instance, in July 1752,

> Benjamin Franklin, Charles Witting, John Inglis and William Coleman are appointed to a Committee to Consider Closing the Writing School.

This early board doesn't look like it codified its committees. Instead it developed committees of trustees to address pressing strategic topics. They created a flexible and responsive board structure—an approach that might help many boards today. Boards can easily become embedded in their structures. Franklin's board seemed to ask what the pressing strategic issues of the day were and how best to organize board work to deal with them. Responsiveness—not ossification—was the approach. Then again, when one is trying to set up a novel approach to government (democracy), flexibility and experimentation might be welcomed.

Trusteeship Can Be Difficult Work (and Sometimes Requires Outside Assistance)

Boards, even though well intended, can struggle with some types of work. Take the aforementioned committee working on the rules for the regulation of schools as an example. The minutes from February 23, 1751, note:

> One of the committees appointed at the last meeting . . . to form Rules for the Regulation of the several schools, acquainted the Trustees, that the forming the said Rules, being a Matter of some Difficulty, the Committee desired further time to consider.

The next meeting minutes of April 1751 report continued difficulty by this committee (but at least they were honest). They requested even more time for their work:

> The Committee appointed to draw up Rules for the Regulation of the several schools, not having yet completed the same, they are desired to have their scheme in readings at the next meeting of the Trustees.

This committee again reported back to the board in June 1751 that they still needed more time.

> The Committee for drawing up a Scheme for regulating the Schools, . . . it is expected that they will have the said Scheme ready to lay before the Trustees at their next meeting.

Finally, the September 1751 meeting minutes recorded the conclusion of this overdue effort with some success (or futility, depending on one's views; also note that the phrase "Difficulties in that Matter" was capitalized in the minutes).

> The Committee for forming Rules for the better Regulation of the Schools, having found some Difficulties in that Matter, proposed to the Trustees to get a Translation made of a Pamphlet written in the German Language . . . containing the Rules and Orders observed in the celebrated [unreadable] School at Kall in Saxony, which being formed upon many years of Experience. . . . Which Proposal was unanimously agreed to and the Committee are desired to get the Pamphlet translated accordingly.

The lesson for today's boards: First, persist. Then recognize your shortcomings and, when stuck, obtain outside counsel (but do so in a language preferably that does not require translation). At least this board seemed to give it the old college try before there was such a thing as an "old college."

Engage With Students, at Appropriate Levels

Today many trustees often feel they are too distant from the life of the campus and the experience of students. Take the advice offered from these colonial trustees:

> It is hoped and expected that the Trustees will make it their Pleasure and in some Degree their Business, to visit the Academy often; to encourage and countenance the youth. . . . And when they have behaved well, gone through their studies and are to enter the World, they shall zealously write and make all the Interest that can be made, to promote and establish them, whether in business, offices, marriages or other things for their Advantage, preferable to all other Persons whatsoever, even of equal merit.

It is interesting to see that this early board encouraged trustee engagement with students first for personally rewarding reasons, and only second for "some degree their business." It is a warning for trustees to have a presence on campus but to know their role as trustees, which has limits and does not include management, and thus the "some degree" qualifier.

Second, as this quotation reminds us, trustees should do what they can to help their graduates to thrive upon leaving the campus. The message here is that the impact of the education they oversee extends beyond the time students are enrolled.

Lessons Beyond the Minutes

This chapter would be remiss if it only focused on the positive lessons. These colonial trustees have other lessons to tell.

First, the names listed in the Constitution and the board meeting minutes—names such as Richard, Abram, Thomas, William, Benjamin, and Sam—suggest that these peers of our Founding Fathers were all men. Men still outrepresent women on boards of trustees and more progress toward equity will serve boards and the institutions they govern better. Second, these men were likely of English descent. Given the ways that the nation's population has diversified, boards today have the need to become racially and ethnically diverse as well.

Furthermore, this board also seems to have met too frequently. The first year of board meetings minutes report substantive work. And the board agreed in 1751 to meet the second Tuesday of every month. Yet, the substance of and attendance at meetings seems to wane as the academy moved into operations. Boards can meet too often, which can be as problematic as boards that meet too infrequently.

Conclusion: If the Past Is Prologue

Although there is not much chance that many of today's trustees will also be directly engaged in fighting a war against England or nation-building to the same extent as these colonial trustees, the experiences from 1749 illustrate many parallels and offer lessons for today. The board meeting minutes from Penn's precursor academy allow not only a glimpse into the past but into the current state of university governance also. They offer insightful and sharp reminders, even if the language is a bit clunky.

In what ways can these minutes also prepare trustees for the future? First, many of the challenges of governance extend beyond the context of history. Governance is hard work and complex and getting it right once does not mean that the challenges will not resurface again.

Second, ensuring sustained and consistent engagement is difficult (shaming and fines didn't work then and most likely won't work now). Building boards that include dedicated and thoughtful individuals requires intentionality and forethought. Doing more to ensure we have the right people in service will lead to stronger boards and better governance.

Finally, governance needs to have its limits, be they term limits (thank you, Mr. Franklin, for your service) or limits on power and reach (interacting with students "in some degree their Business"). All of these factors can be lessons readily applied to today's and, likely, to tomorrow's college and university boards.

Questions for Boards

1. To what extent are your board meetings, like Franklin's, expected to be debates and not rubber stamps?
2. Like Franklin's board, how flexible and responsive are your committee structures?
3. How well do you address issues of risk?
4. What is the culture of philanthropy on your board? How does it compare to Franklin's?

5. To what extent does your board remind itself "that the Trustees will make it their Pleasure and in some Degree their Business, to visit the Academy often?" (Remember that the recommendation is some "degree of business," as a warning against too much board intrusion through too many visits.)

For Further Insight

To follow up on some of the issues raised in this chapter, we suggest:

- Chapter 3: Is Your Board Mediocre?
- Chapter 4: Individual Competencies for Collective Impact
- Chapter 5: Right Answers; Wrong Questions
- Chapter 7: Ensuring Accountability for the Board by the Board
- Chapter 9: The "Jobs" of Committees: Of Drill Bits and Milkshakes

16½

HALF A CHAPTER
The Unfinished Work

As the chapters in this volume demonstrate, governance is a constant work in progress. Boards must keep working toward improvement and being intentional about their work. So why label the conclusion only half a chapter? We do this because the ideas in this book tell only part of the story. The rest remains to be written by each board as it moves into the future. The completion of the chapter is the ongoing work of the board, its leaders, and the administration with which it partners. We invite you to draft the remainder of this chapter through the work you do, the questions about governance you pose, and the intentionality and tenacity that you demonstrate.

A Work in Progress

Although boards are often encouraged to get governance right, the problem with this goal is that governance is an ongoing work in progress. The issues change, as do the participants. The context shifts and so does board culture. The idea of getting governance right suggests that governance is static—that there is an end-state suggesting a right way. The reality in boardrooms is that stasis doesn't happen. The target is moving, and a steady or fixed state—when it comes to governance—means stagnation. The idea of getting governance "right" suggests that someone can tell a board what governance is "right"— that there is a best way. Effective governance cannot be prescribed or dictated; it is contextual, and the most helpful answer to a question about governance might well be "let's think about that." Governance isn't something to get right but something that continues to progress and that takes effort.

This book ends with a request for you and your board to write the second half of this chapter. Only an individual board can write what is next for it. This book asks boards to approach their work as evolutionary, and for some, revolutionary (particularly if you have one of those mediocre boards). Boards will write this chapter based on how they continue to think about and evolve governance, and how they act in accordance.

Throughout this book we have stressed that governance that adds value requires intentionality, insight, foresight, and commitment. Governance at too many institutions "just happens." Instead, we want governance to happen well, and to do so repeatedly and over time. Better boards ask themselves questions and adopt that "positive restlessness" (Kuh et al., 2005, p. 46) about their work that has been mentioned previously.

We framed this book as a way to help boards think more intentionally about various aspects of governance. Thinking differently, we propose, is the precursor to acting differently. We wanted to provide boards with tools, but ones different from the standard "how-to-govern-best" fare. Thus, both thought and action are the tools for better governing.

Preparing for the Future

We think of governance as dynamic—because the future of higher education and of each institution and state system is also dynamic—but with important nuance. To drive this point home, we sometimes ask boards to describe what is most interesting about the following headlines from the *Chronicle of Higher Education* (higher education's version of the *Wall Street Journal*).

- Students' Borrowing Quintuples in Decade
- Higher Education Losing Credibility in Congress
- Quest to Make U.S. More Competitive Could Be a Boon to Higher Education
- Part-Time Teachers Turn to Unions to Alter Status as "Academic Stepchildren"
- Peer Review Under Scrutiny by Government Agencies
- Trying to End Sports Woes at U
- [Foreign Power] Set to Start Ambitious Reform of Educational System

Responses typically focus on the negativity of the headlines, the external demands and expectations of higher education, the complexity and interrelations of the issues, the importance of public perception, questions about higher education's financial well-being, and higher education's status as a troubled industry responding to many masters.

Although all keen observations, boards (as well as administrators) are surprised to learn that these headlines are from 1987. What does it tell us that these issues are as relevant today as they were more than three decades ago? It suggests to us three things as boards think about the future and how best to ensure that governance evolves.

First, the future will include a continuation of current and even past issues and challenges. Second, the future will include the unanticipated and the unexpected. These are the unknowns that we cannot predict or for which we cannot necessarily prepare. Third, the future includes the anticipated and the projected. This is the group of issues that capture most conversations about the future. How can we see around the corner or peer over the horizon? In reality, boards need to prepare themselves and their institutions to address all three trajectories.

The work of boards for the future is threefold. Boards need to focus on the hard work necessary for progress and organize themselves accordingly (see chapter 9 on the "jobs" of committees and chapter 13 on "trying issues," for examples). For known trends and issues, boards should invest the time and develop the capacity to look ahead. They should be intentional about preparing the institutions and themselves for the future. For the unknowns, boards should work to develop the capacity for uncertainty and ambiguity and recognize the challenges and discomfort with that work (see Table 16.5.1). As former secretary of defense Donald Rumsfeld (2002) said, there are "known unknowns" and "unknown unknowns."

In the future, boards will increasingly be called upon to define and evolve their governance work because they will rarely be handed a well-crafted problem to solve. The world moves too quickly, the challenges are too complex, and the factors are too uncertain.

TABLE 16.5.1
Board Work for the Future

Future Is. . .	The Board's Work
Continuation of the ongoing	Focus on the hard work and organize for progress
Known	Invest time and develop the capacity to look ahead and understand the implications for the institution or system and the board
Unknown	Develop the capacity for the uncertain and ambiguous

As scholar Donald Schön (1983) wrote, reflective practitioners must engage in "problem setting,"

> the process by which we define the decisions to be made, the ends to be achieved, and the means which may be chosen. In real-world practice, problems do not present themselves to the practitioner as givens. They must be constructed from the material of problematic situations which are puzzling, troubling, and uncertain. In order to convert a problematic situation to a problem, a practitioner must do a certain kind of work. He [*sic*] must make sense of an uncertain situation that initially makes no sense. (p. 40)

The work of the future is just that, making sense where there at first is no sense and developing the capacity to move ahead pragmatically. This sensemaking, over time, is what great boards do. On that note, we really like Christian Madsbjerg's (2017) five principles for sensemaking:

1. Focus on understanding the collective culture—*not* individuals, getting at *why* people act the way they do as part of a group.
2. Use thick data—*not* just thin data. Sensemaking requires information and data that is contextualized; getting at what is meaningful about a culture requires not just fact, but also context.
3. Consider the savannah—*not* the zoo. Sensemaking requires getting at the real, lived experience—at eye level, not a contrived view from a distance.
4. Think creativity—*not* manufacturing. Sensemaking is more inductive than deductive; it requires "the type of thinking that leads to all creative insights: filled with twists and turns, dead ends, and unexplained breakthroughs" (p. 21).
5. Find the North Star—*not* the GPS. "We are so fixated on staring at the oracle of the GPS that we have lost all sensitivity of the stars right above our heads" (p. 22).

As boards make sense of the unfolding future, they are well served to work to understand that which may be invisible (culture—on the board and at the institution); use "thick data" (not just that which is easy to capture, but that which provides meaning); gain a sense of how people (students, faculty, and staff) experience the campus and programs; think critically, convergently, and inductively; and focus collectively on the institutional North Star (values, mission, vision) rather than getting lost in the details (technical problems).

Conclusion: Writing the Rest

This book is about making boards as effective as they can be and offers ideas to think about structure (board size, committees, number of meetings, policies, and practices); content (what boards spend their time on); and culture (how boards interact; group and power dynamics). This conclusion of the conclusion challenges boards to write the rest of their own chapter on governance. They will do so most likely without pen and paper (or a keyboard), but through reflective work. Your future comes from how your board will continue to challenge itself to keep up with or even get out ahead of governance challenges and expectations. The task of writing is hard work (believe us, we just finished this book), even if it is a metaphor for action. It requires knowing what you want to say, understanding how you want to say what you are going to say, and having the vocabulary to craft and convey your ideas.

Governance, too, is hard work with many parallels to writing. It requires knowing where you want to go, having the desire to bring about change and continue to evolve, mastering the tools to get there, and having the ability to convey the results. Start writing.

Questions for Boards

1. Looking at the past three to five years, how has your board evolved? In what ways are institutional priorities the same or different and to what extent has the work of the board shifted?
2. How much time has the board allocated to discussions about how it works and to governance as a process? Is this time sufficient? How might it increase its appropriate focus on its own work?
3. How can the board create a sense of "positive restlessness" about its own work?
4. What might the board do differently to break out of tired routines?
5. What are the significant contributions the board has made to the institution or system's well-being and how can it ensure that it will do more of this kind of work?
6. Is the board paying attention to all three areas that lead to high performance: content, structure, and culture?

REFERENCES

Addo, K. (2016, February 25). Board of curators fires Mizzou assistant professor Melissa Click. *St. Louis Post Dispatch.* Retrieved from http://www.stltoday.com/news/local/education/board-of-curators-fires-mizzou-assistant-professor-melissa-click/article_d334e896-f16e-52f1-96a4-171da43590ef.html

Alderfer, C. P. (1986). The invisible director on corporate boards. *Harvard Business Review, 64*(6), 38–52.

American Hospital Association. (2009). *Competency-based governance: A foundation for board and organizational effectiveness.* Chicago, IL: Center for Healthcare Governance and Health Research & Educational Trust.

Associated Press (2008, September 16). Michigan State revokes Mugabe's honorary degree. Retrieved from http://diverseeducation.com/article/11685/

Associated Press (2018, April 7). Ohio State revokes Bill Cosby's honorary degree amid retrial. Retrieved from https://www.usatoday.com/story/life/people/2018/04/07/ohio-state-revokes-bill-cosbys-honorary-degree-amid-retrial/495901002/

Association of Governing Boards of Universities and Colleges. (2010). *AGB statement on board responsibility for institutional governance.* Washington, DC: AGB.

Association of Governing Boards of Universities and Colleges. (2013). *AGB statement on conflict of interest and compelling benefits.* Washington DC: AGB.

Association of Governing Boards of Universities and Colleges. (2015a). *The AGB directors' statement on the fiduciary duties of governing board members.* Washington DC: AGB. Retrieved from https://www.agb.org/sites/default/files/u27174/statement_2015_fiduciary_duties.pdf

Association of Governing Boards of Universities and Colleges. (2015b). *Consequential boards: Adding value where it matters most* (Report of the National Commission on College and University Board Governance). Washington DC: AGB.

Association of Governing Boards of Universities and Colleges. (2016). *Policies, practices and composition of governing and foundation boards 2016.* Washington DC: AGB.

Baldridge, J. V. (1971). *Power and conflict in the university: Research in the sociology of complex organizations.* New York, NY: Wiley.

Beinart, P. (2017, March 6). A violent attack on free speech at Middlebury. *The Atlantic.* Retrieved from https://www.theatlantic.com/politics/archive/2017/03/middlebury-free-speech-violence/518667/

Berger, W. (2014). *A more beautiful question: The power of inquiry to spark breakthrough ideas.* New York, NY: Bloomsbury.

Berlin, I. (1953). *The hedgehog and the fox.* Chicago, IL: Elephant.

Birnbaum, R. (1988). *How colleges work: The cybernetics of academic organization and leadership.* San Francisco, CA: Jossey-Bass.

Birnbaum, R. (1989). The latent organizational functions of the academic senate. *The Journal of Higher Education, 60*(4), 423–443.

Birnbaum, R. (1992, January/February). Will you love me in December as you do in May?: Why experienced college presidents lose faculty support. *The Journal of Higher Education, 63*(1), 1–25.

Birnbaum, R. (2001). *Management fads in higher education: Where they come from, what they do, why they fail.* San Francisco, CA: Jossey-Bass.

Birnbaum, R. (2004a). *Speaking for higher education.* Newport, CT: Praeger.

Birnbaum, R. (2004b). *The end of shared governance: Looking ahead or looking back.* Retrieved from https://pullias.usc.edu/wp-content/uploads/2014/06/the-end-of-shared-governance.pdf

Bolman, L. G., & Deal, T. E. (2017). *Reframing organizations: Artistry, choice and leadership* (6th ed.). New York, NY: Wiley.

Bowen, W. G. (1994, September/October). When a business leader joins a non-profit board. *Harvard Business Review, 72*(5), 38–44.

Bowen, W. G., & Tobin, E. M. (2015). *Locus of authority: The evolution of faculty roles in the governance of higher education.* Princeton, NJ: Princeton University Press and ITHAKA.

Boyd, B. K., Takacs Haynes, K., & Zona, F. (2011). Dimensions of CEO-board relations. *Journal of Management Studies, 48*(8), 1892–1923.

Bregman, P. (2013, January). A personal approach to organizational time management. *McKinsey Quarterly.* Retrieved from https://www.mckinsey.com/business-functions/organization/our-insights/a-personal-approach-to-organizational-time-management

Brooks, D. (2010, April 8). The humble hound. *New York Times* [Op-Ed]. Retrieved from http://www.nytimes.com/2010/04/09/opinion/09brooks.html

Calhoun, L. (2017, May 15). Elon Musk on the 1 creative skill every founder needs now. *Inc.* Retrieved from https://www.inc.com/lisa-calhoun/elon-musk-on-the-1-creative-skill-every-founder-needs-now.html

Casteen, J. T. (2015, July/August). Learning from Sweet Briar. *Trusteeship, 23*(4), 28–31.

Cerna, L. (2014). *Trust: What it is and why it matters for governance and education* (OECD Education Working Papers No. 108). Paris, France: OECD.

Chait, R. (2000, November/December). Trustees & professors: So often at odds, so much alike. *Trusteeship, 8*(6), 8-12.

Chait, R. (2006, May/June). Why good boards go bad. *Trusteeship, 14*(3), 1–4.

Chait, R. (2009, July/August). The gremlins of governance. *Trusteeship, 17*(4), 8–13.

Chait, R. (2016, May/June). The bedrock of board culture. *Trusteeship, 24*(3), 20–24.

Chait, R. P., Ryan, W. P., & Taylor B. E. (2005). *Governance as leadership: Reframing the work of nonprofit boards.* Hoboken, NJ: Wiley.

Charan, R. (2005). *Boards that deliver: Advancing corporate governance from compliance to competitive advantage.* San Francisco, CA: Jossey-Bass.

Christensen, C., Cook, S., & Hall, T. (2005, December). Marketing malpractice: The cause and the cure. *Harvard Business Review.* Retrieved from https://hbr.org/2005/12/marketing-malpractice-the-cause-and-the-cure

Cohen, M. D., & March, J. G. (1986). *Leadership and ambiguity: The American college president.* Boston, MA: Harvard Business School Press.

Collins, J. (2005). *Good to great and the social sectors.* Boulder, CO: Jim Collins.

Committee of University Chairs. (2014, December). *The Higher Education Code of Governance.* Retrieved from http://www.universitychairs.ac.uk/wp-content/uploads/2015/02/Code-Final.pdf

Cone, A. (2017, April 24). Students to sue UC Berkeley for canceling Coulter's speech. UPI. Retrieved from https://www.upi.com/Students-to-sue-UC-Berkeley-for-canceling-Coulters-speech/2451492952203/

Covey, S. R. (1989). *The 7 habits of highly effective people.* New York, NY: Simon & Schuster.

De Jong, B. A., Dirks, K. T., & Gillespie, N. (2016). Trust and team performance: A meta-analysis of main effects, moderators, and covariates. *Journal of Applied Psychology, 101*(8), 1134–1150.

Dimeo, J. (2017, October 4). Marketing strategies in overdrive. *Inside Higher Ed.* Retrieved from https://www.insidehighered.com/digital-learning/article/2017/10/04/how-colleges-market-online-courses-and-programs

Dowling, D. W. (2009, September). Bain & Company chairman Orit Gadiesh on the importance of curiosity. *Harvard Business Review.* Retrieved from https://hbr.org/2009/09/bain-company-chairman-orit-gadiesh-on-the-importance-of-curiosity

Drucker, P. F. (1990). *Managing the non-profit organization: Principles and practices.* New York, NY: HarperCollins.

Eckel, P. D. (2009). *Changing course: Making the hard decisions to eliminate academic programs,* (2nd ed.). Lanham, MD: Rowman & Littlefield Publishers.

Eckel, P. D. (2013, November/December). What presidents really think about their boards. *Trusteeship, 21*(6), 6–13.

Eckel, P. D. (2014a, May 13). A letter to new presidents [Web log post]. *AGB.* Retrieved from https://www.agb.org/blog/2014/05/13/a-letter-to-new-presidents

Eckel, P. D. (2014b, May 15). A letter to board members upon hiring a new president [Web log post]. *AGB.* Retrieved from https://www.agb.org/blog/2014/05/15/a-letter-to-board-members-upon-hiring-a-new-president

Eckel, P. D., & Trower, C. (2016, November). *Boards and institutional diversity: Missed opportunities, points of leverage.* New York, NY: TIAA Institute. Retrieved from https://www.tiaainstitute.org/sites/default/files/presentations/2017-02/boards_and_institutional_diversity.pdf

French, J. R. P., Jr., & Raven, B. H. (1959). The bases of social power. In D. Cartwright (Ed.), *Studies in social power* (pp. 150–167). Ann Arbor, MI: Institute for Social Research.

Friedersdorf, C. (2016, March 24). A dialogue on race and speech at Yale. Retrieved from https://www.theatlantic.com/politics/archive/2016/03/yale-silliman-race/475152/

Gearty, R. (1998, November 18). Adelphi settles suit. *New York Daily News*. Retrieved from http://beta.nydailynews.com/archives/boroughs/adelphi-settles-suit-article-1.804396

Gioia, D. A., and Thomas, J. B. (1996). Identity, image and issue interpretation: Sensemaking during strategic change in academia. *Administrative Science Quarterly, 41*(3), 370–403.

Gluck, F. W., Kaufman, S. P., Walleck, A. S., McLeod, K., & Stuckey, J. (2000, June). Thinking strategically. *McKinsey Quarterly*. Retrieved from https://www.mckinsey.com/business-functions/strategy-and-corporate-finance/our-insights/thinking-strategically

Grant, A. (2016). *Originals: How non-conformists move the world*. New York, NY: Penguin.

Groysberg, B., Lee, J., Price, J., & Yo-Jud Cheng, J. (2018, January/February). The leader's guide to corporate culture. *Harvard Business Review, 96*(1), 44–57.

Harper, S. R., & Harris, F., III. (2012). *Men of Color: A role for policymakers in improving the status of Black male students in U.S. higher education*. Washington DC: Institute for Higher Education Policy.

Harris, A. (2017, December 5). Moody's downgrades higher ed's outlook from 'stable' to 'negative.' *Chronicle of Higher Education*. Retrieved from https://www.chronicle.com/article/Moody-s-Downgrades-Higher/241983

Harris, E. A. (2015, April 10). Cooper Union offers to let president go as part of deal with state attorney general. *New York Times*. Retrieved from https://www.nytimes.com/2015/04/11/nyregion/cooper-union-offers-to-let-president-go-as-part-of-deal-with-state-attorney-general.html

Harrison, S. (2011). Organizing the cat? Generative aspects of curiosity in organizational life. In G. M. Spreitzer and K. S. Cameron (Eds.), *The Oxford handbook of positive organizational scholarship* (pp. 110–124). Oxford, UK: Oxford University Press.

Hartocollis, A. (2017, July 9). *Long after protests, students shun the University of Missouri*. Retrieved from https://www.nytimes.com/2017/07/09/us/university-of-missouri-enrollment-protests-fallout.html

Heifetz, R. (1994). *Leadership without easy answers*. Cambridge, MA: The Belknap Press of Harvard University Press.

Hildreth, J. A. D., & Anderson, C. (2016). Failure at the top: How power undermines collaborative performance. *Journal of Personality and Social Psychology, 110*(2), 261–286.

Hobson, W. (2017, December 28). Six years later, Penn State remains torn over the Sandusky scandal. *The Washington Post*. Retrieved from https://www.washingtonpost.com/graphics/2017/sports/penn-state-six-years-after-sandusky-scandal/?utm_term=.caa435753f94

Internal Revenue Service. 2017. *Form 990*. Retrieved from https://www.irs.gov/pub/irs-pdf/f990.pdf

Janis, I. L. (1973). Groupthink and group dynamics: A social psychological analysis of policy decisions. *Policy Studies Journal, (2)*1, 19–25.

Jaschik, S. (2016, February 1). Standing with their president. *Inside Higher Ed.* Retrieved from https://www.insidehighered.com/news/2016/02/01/suffolk-u-board-moves-fire-president-despite-her-backing-students-professors-and

Jaschik, S. (2016, March 1). President quits at Mount St. Mary's. *Inside Higher Ed.* Retrieved from https://www.insidehighered.com/news/2016/03/01/president-quits-mount-st-marys

Jaschik, S. (2017, October 9). Who counts as a black student? *Inside Higher Ed.* Retrieved from https://www.insidehighered.com/admissions/article/2017/10/09/cornell-students-revive-debate-whom-colleges-should-count-black

Jenkins, S. (2018, March 2). Commentary: Michigan State's problems start much higher than Larry Nassar and sports coaches. *The Washington Post.* Retrieved from http://www.chicagotribune.com/sports/college/ct-spt-michigan-state-larry-nassar-sally-jenkins-20180302-story.html

Kahn, G. (2014, January 2). The amazon of higher education. *Slate.* Retrieved from http://www.slate.com/articles/life/education/2014/01/southern_new_hampshire_university_how_paul_leblanc_s_tiny_school_has_become.html

Kahneman, D. (2011). *Thinking fast and slow.* New York, NY: Farrar, Straus, and Giroux.

Knich, D. & Smith, G. (2012, May 6). A university in crisis: Saving South Carolina State. *The Post and Courier.* Retrieved from https://www.postandcourier.com/archives/a-university-in-crisis-saving-south-carolina-stategreene-column-s/article_0d4065f0-00ef-55c1-b02d-21015338c6e2.html

Kramer, R. A. (2010). Collective trust within organizations: Conceptual foundations and empirical insights. *Corporate Reputation Review, 13*(2), 82–97.

Kuh, G. D., Kinzie, J., Schuh, J. H., & Whitt, E. J. (2005, July/August). Never let it rest: Lessons about student success and high-performing colleges and universities. *Change, 37*(4), 44–51.

Lafley, A. G., & Martin, R. L. (2013). *Playing to win: How strategy really works.* Boston, MA: Harvard Business School Publishing.

Leonard, H. (2013, September 30). *The four accountabilities in governance of social enterprises.* Speech at the Summit of Nonprofit Board Leadership, San Francisco, CA. Retrieved from http://hbscp.org/wp-content/uploads/2013/10/Four-Accountabilities-HBS-GSB-Alumni-SF-CA-2013-09-30-for-pdf-copy.pdf

Lerner, J. S., & Tetlock, P. E. (1999). Accounting for the effects of accountability. *Psychological Bulletin, 125*(2), 2255–2275.

Lerner, J. S., & Tetlock, P. E. (2002). Bridging individual, interpersonal, and institutional approaches to judgment and choice: The impact of accountability on cognitive bias. In S. Schneider & J. Shanteau (Eds.), *Emerging perspectives in judgment and decision making* (pp. 431–457). Cambridge, UK: Cambridge University Press.

Litman, J. (2005). Curiosity and the pleasures of learning: Wanting and liking new information. *Cognition and Emotion, 19*(6), 793–814.

Lublin, J. (2014, August 26). Small boards get bigger returns. *Wall Street Journal*. Retrieved from https://www.wsj.com/articles/smaller-boards-get-bigger-returns-1409078628

Madsbjerg, C. (2017). *Sensemaking: The power of the humanities in the age of the algorithm*. New York, NY: Hachette Books.

March, J. (1994). *A primer on decision making: How decisions happen*. New York, NY: Free Press.

Marcus, J. (2015a, March 11). Is Arizona State University the model for the new American university? *Hechinger Report*. Retrieved from http://hechingerreport.org/is-arizona-state-university-the-model-for-the-new-american-university/

Marcus, J. (2015b, April 30). Once invisible, college boards of trustees are suddenly in the spotlight. *The Hechinger Report*. Retrieved from http://hechingerreport.org/once-invisible-college-boards-of-trustees-are-suddenly-in-the-spotlight/

Martin, J. (2002). *Organizational culture*. Thousand Oaks, CA: Sage.

Martin, R. L. (2010, July/August). The execution trap. *Harvard Business Review*, *86*(7–8), 64–71, 168.

Martin, R. L (2014, January/February). The big lie of strategic planning. *Harvard Business Review*, *92*(1/2), 79–84.

Martin, R. L. (2015, May 5). The first question to ask of any strategy. *Harvard Business Review*. Retrieved from https://hbr.org/2015/05/the-first-question-to-ask-of-any-strategy

McFarlan, F. W. (1999, November/December). Working on nonprofit boards: Don't assume the shoe fits. *Harvard Business Review*, *77*(6), 64–80.

McNulty, T., Pettigrew, A., Jobome, G., & Morris, C. (2011). The role, power and influence of company chairs. *Journal of Management & Governance*, *15*, 91–121.

Merriam-Webster's Collegiate Dictionary. (1999). Tenth edition. Springfield, MA: Merriam-Webster, Incorporated.

Miller, J. R. (2018, January 26). Michigan State's sexual assault problem spreads to football, basketball. *New York Post*. Retrieved from https://nypost.com/2018/01/26/michigan-states-sexual-assault-problem-isnt-limited-to-nassar/

Minor, J. T. (2003). Assessing the senate: critical issues considered. *American Behavioral Scientist*, *46*(7), 960–977.

Minor, J. T. (2004). Understanding faculty senates: Moving from mystery to models. *The Review of Higher Education*, *27*(3), 343–363.

Mintzberg, H. (1983) *Structure in fives: Designing effective organizations*, Englewood Cliffs, NJ: Prentice-Hall.

Mintzberg, H. (2007). *Tracking strategies: Toward a general theory of strategy formation*. New York, NY: Oxford University Press.

Moltz, D. (2009, June 17). Trustee troubles. *Inside Higher Ed*. Retrieved from https://www.insidehighered.com/news/2009/06/17/rogue

Montgomery, C. (2012, July). How strategists lead. *McKinsey Quarterly*. Retrieved from https://www.mckinsey.com/business-functions/strategy-and-corporate-finance/our-insights/how-strategists-lead

Moody's Investor Services (2013, January 16). Retrieved from https://www.moodys.com/research/Moodys-2013-outlook-for-entire-US-Higher-Education-sector-changed--PR_263866#

Moody's Investor Services (2015, July 20). Retrieved from https://www.moodys.com/research/Moodys-US-higher-education-outlook-revised-to-stable-as-revenues--PR_330530

Pappano, L. (2017, August 4). More diversity means more demands. Retrieved from https://www.nytimes.com/2017/08/04/education/edlife/protests-claremont-college-student-demands.html

Pearce, J. A. II, & Zahra, S. A. (1992). Board composition from a strategic management perspective. *Journal of Management Studies, 29*(3), 411–438.

Popova, M. (2012, June 8). Frank Lloyd Wright's thoughts on learning. *The Atlantic.* Retrieved from https://www.theatlantic.com/entertainment/archive/2012/06/frank-lloyd-wrights-thoughts-on-learning/258286/

Porter, M. E. (1996, November/December). What is strategy? *Harvard Business Review, 74*(6), 61–78.

Prybil, L. D. (2006). Size, composition, and culture of high-performing hospital boards. *American Journal of Medical Quality, 21*(4), 224–229.

Quenk, N. L. (2001). *Essentials of Myers-Briggs Type Indicator Assessment.* New York, NY: Wiley.

Raven, B. H. (2008). The bases of power and the power/interaction model of interpersonal influence. *Analysis of Social Issues and Public Policy, 8*(1), 1–22.

Reich, R. (2013, April 22). *Education for a competitive future.* Keynote speech at the Association of Governing Boards National Conference on Trusteeship. San Francisco, CA.

Rocheleau, M. (2015, January 29). Dartmouth bans hard alcohol, forbids Greek life pledging. *Boston Globe.* Retrieved from https://www.bostonglobe.com/metro/2015/01/29/dartmouth-college-ban-hard-alcohol-forbid-greek-life-pledging-among-slew-policy-changes/WCxS4OHSLK5hZ5Z7u5E8iN/story.html

Rumsfeld, D. (2002, February 12). U.S. Department of Defense (DoD) news briefing. Retrieved from https://opinionator.blogs.nytimes.com/2014/03/25/the-certainty-of-donald-rumsfeld-part-1/

Russell Reynolds Associates. (2009). *Different is better—Why diversity matters in the boardroom.* Retrieved from http://www.russellreynolds.com/insights/thought-leadership/different-is-better-why-diversity-matters-in-the-boardroom

Savidge, N. (2016, May 3). UW-Madison faculty declare 'no confidence' in board of regents, UW system president. *Michigan State Journal.* Retrieved from http://host.madison.com/wsj/news/local/education/university/uw-madison-faculty-declare-no-confidence-in-board-of-regents/article_bf7e7864-7ea6-54f1-8dfc-edbba2e14c59.html

Sawyer, K. (2007). *Group genius: The creative power of collaboration.* New York, NY: Basic Books.

Schein, E. H. (1992). *Organizational culture and leadership* (2nd ed.). San Francisco, CA: Jossey-Bass.

Schön, D. A. (1983). *The reflective practitioner: How professionals think in action.* New York, NY: Basic Books.

Schwarz, R. (2013, July 15). Increase your team's curiosity. *Harvard Business Review.* Retrieved from https://hbr.org/2013/07/increase-your-teams-curiosity

Shen, W. (2003). The dynamics of the CEO-board relationship: An evolutionary perspective. *Academy of Management Review, 28*(3), 466–476.

Sinek, S. (2009). *Start with why: How great leaders inspire everyone to take action.* New York, NY: Portfolio/Penguin.

Sleesman, D. J., Conlon, D. E., McNamara, G., & Miles, J. E. (2012). Cleaning up the big muddy: A meta-analytic review of the determinants of escalation of commitment. *Academy of Management Journal, 55*(3), 541–562.

Sonnenfeld, J. A. (2002). What makes great boards great. *Harvard Business Review, 80*(9), 106–113.

Straumsheim, C. (2017, March 21). The unbundling university. *Inside Higher Ed.* Retrieved from https://www.insidehighered.com/news/2017/03/21/u-maryland-university-college-pursues-strategy-unbundling

Stripling, J. (2012, August 20). Rehired as UVa president, Sullivan aims to 'reset' relations with board. *Chronicle of Higher Education.* Retrieved from https://www.chronicle.com/article/Rehired-as-UVa-President/133796

Stripling, J. (2017, August 17). At UVa, a clash over whether to stand back or stand up. *Chronicle of Higher Education.* Retrieved from https://www.chronicle.com/article/At-UVa-a-Clash-Over-Whether/240952

Sunstein, C. R., & Hastie, R. (2015). *Wiser: Getting beyond groupthink to make groups smarter.* Boston, MA: Harvard Business Review Press.

Tetlock, P. E. (2005). *Expert political judgment: How good is it? How can we know?* Princeton, NJ: Princeton University Press.

Troop, D. (2014, July 14). Moody's issues negative outlook for higher education. *Chronical of Higher Education.* https://www.chronicle.com/blogs/bottomline/moodys-issues-negative-outlook-for-higher-education/

Trower, C. A. (2013). *The practitioner's guide to governance as leadership: Building high-performing nonprofit boards.* San Francisco, CA: Jossey-Bass.

Trower, C. A. (2015, March/April). Flipping the boardroom for trustee engagement: Why and how. *Trusteeship, 23*(2), 25–29.

Ubell, R. (2017, November 21). How online can save small, private colleges from going under. *EdSurge.* Retrieved from https://www.edsurge.com/news/2017-11-21-how-online-can-save-small-private-colleges-from-going-under

University of Pennsylvania (1749-1768). Minutes of the Trustees of the College, Academy and Charitable Schools Vol 1. 1749-1768. University of Pennsylvania Archives. Retrieved from the University Library and Archives http://sceti.library.upenn.edu/sceti/codex/public/PageLevel/index.cfm?WorkID=787

Walker, D. E. (1979). *The effective administrator.* San Francisco, CA: Jossey-Bass.

Watkins, M. (2016, August 19). After athletics scandal, Ken Starr leaves Baylor faculty. *The Texas Tribune.* Retrieved from https://www.texastribune.org/2016/08/19/after-athletics-scandal-ken-starr-leaves-baylor-fa/

Weick, K. E. (1976, March). Educational organizations as loosely coupled systems. *Administrative Science Quarterly, 21*(1), 1–19.

Weick, K. E. (1982). Management of organizational chance among loosely coupled elements. In P. S. Goodman & Associates (Eds.), *Change in organizations* (pp. 375–408). San Francisco, CA: Jossey-Bass.

Weick, K. E. (1995). *Sensemaking in organizations.* Thousand Oaks, CA: Sage.

Westphal, J. D. (1999). Collaboration in the boardroom: Behavioral and performance consequences of CEO–board social ties. *Academy of Management Journal, 42*(1), 7–24.

Wexler, E. (2016, February 19). On the hook in Louisiana. *Inside Higher Ed.* Retrieved from https://www.insidehighered.com/news/2016/02/19/la-freezes-payments-state-grant-program-colleges-pick-slack

YMCA (2009/2010). *Developing cause-driven leaders: Leadership competency development guide.* Retrieved from http://www.mcgawymca.org/main/wp-content/uploads/2013/01/Leadership-Competency-Development-Guide.pdf

ABOUT THE AUTHORS

Peter D. Eckel serves as senior fellow and director of leadership programs at the Alliance for Higher Education and Democracy (AHEAD) in the University of Pennsylvania's Graduate School of Education. His expertise focuses on managing and governing colleges and universities. He teaches in both the executive doctorate program in higher education management and the traditional higher education graduate program. He also provides consultation to and develops executive leadership programs for trustees, presidents, provosts, senior student affairs executives, and other campus leaders, both domestically and internationally.

Previously, he was the vice president for programs and research at the Association of Governing Boards of Universities and Colleges (AGB). Among other efforts, he developed AGB's Presidential Initiative and oversaw its consulting services. He worked for 16 years at the American Council on Education (ACE), finishing his tenure as director of the Center for Effective Leadership. At ACE, he led the development of its suite of senior leadership programs and was the founding director of the ACE Institute for New Chief Academic Officers, the Advancing to the Presidency Workshop, and the ACE Presidential Roundtable Series.

Eckel has written/edited six books prior to this one, including *Changing Course: Making the Hard Decisions to Eliminate Academic Programs* (Rowman & Littlefield, 2009); *Privatizing the Public University: Perspectives From Across the Academy* (with Christopher Morphew; Johns Hopkins University Press, 2009); and *Taking the Reins: Institutional Transformation in Higher Education* (with Adrianna Kezar; American Council on Education and Praeger, 2003). He has written 24 nationally disseminated papers, including "Presidential Leadership in an Age of Transition"; "Finding the Right Prescription for Higher Education's Ills: Can Health Care Provide Answers"; and ACE's *On Change* series. He was the lead author of the *CAO Census*, the first national study of chief academic officers.

He earned his doctorate from the University of Maryland, College Park, in education policy, planning, and administration. He was recognized in 2011 as the Thomas Magoon Distinguished Alumni Award recipient from the Department of Counseling and Personnel Services from which he received his master's degree. His bachelor's degree is in journalism from

Michigan State University. He currently serves as a trustee at the University of La Verne (California) where he sits on the enrollment, academic and student affairs, and finance committees.

Cathy A. Trower is president of Trower & Trower, Inc. (www.trowerand trower.com), a board governance consulting firm, through which she has provided consulting and coaching services to more than 170 nonprofits, including dozens of colleges and universities. Trower is author of *The Practitioner's Guide to Governance as Leadership: Building High-Performing Nonprofit Boards* (Jossey-Bass, 2013) and the second edition of *Govern More, Manage Less* (BoardSource, 2010). She is coauthor with R. Barbara Gitenstein of *What Board Members Need to Know About Faculty* (Association of Governing Boards of Universities and Colleges, 2013), and she has written several articles for the AGB's *Trusteeship* magazine—most recently, "Flipping the Boardroom for Trustee Engagement: Why and How" (March/April 2015).

Formerly research director at the Harvard Graduate School of Education, Trower studied academic leadership, shared governance, faculty work life, employment issues, policies, and practices including the experiences of faculty through a generational lens, women in STEM disciplines, and underrepresented minorities for 16 years. Prior to Harvard, Trower served as a senior-level administrator of business degree programs at Johns Hopkins University; she has also been a faculty member and department chair at a liberal arts college. Trower has published an edited volume on faculty policies as well as dozens of book chapters, articles, and case studies.

Trower is chair of the BoardSource (Washington DC) Board of Directors and vice chair and governance chair of the RiverWoods Continuing Care Retirement Community (Exeter, New Hampshire) Board of Trustees. Formerly, she served as trustee and vice chair of the Governance Committee at Wheaton College (Massachusetts).

Trower has a BBA (1981) and an MBA (1985) from the University of Iowa and a PhD (1996) in education policy, planning, and administration from the University of Maryland, College Park.

education for, 89–90
engagement problems with, 12, 62
expectations of, 39
faculty commonalties with, 170–71
faculty communication with, 30, 31
financial support from, 175–76
frustration from, 123, 144–45
homework for, 39–40, 63, 65
insight from, 145–46
media judgment of, 25
mediocrity of, 35–36
meeting perspectives from, 60–61
orientation for, 45–46
power imbalance among, 123, 124–25, 126–29
public shaming of, 177
rogue, 46–47
role of, 2
routine break for, 87
statement of expectations for, 80
strategies for preparedness of, 70–71
with strategy experience, 159
unfamiliar issues addressed by, 29
as volunteers, 4, 24–25, 29
tuition-dependence, 98
tuition discounting, 29

underperformance. *See also* mediocrity
board culture influencing, 106–7

of governing boards, 5, 7, 33–34, 52
reasons for, 34–38
United Kingdom, 78
Unite the Right campaign, 140–41
University of Cincinnati, 95
University of Michigan, 95, 96
University of Missouri, 25, 142
University of Pennsylvania
academy's constitution of, 174
colonial board of, 9, 173
University of Vermont's College of Education and Social Services, 155–57
University of Virginia, 31, 140–41

virtual meeting, 54
volunteers
evaluation of selves, 38–39
trustees as, 4, 24–25, 29
vulnerability. *See* strengths/ vulnerabilities

Wheaton College
agenda for, 63, 64–65, 66–67
committee restructuring for, 99
wisdom
defined, 2
from experience, 136
in governing boards, 10
women presidents, 135, 138

an urgent need for leadership that is conversant with, and able to deploy, the competencies, management tools, and strategic skills that go beyond the technical or disciplinary preparation and on-the-job training that most leaders have received.

This book is intended as a practical resource for academic and administrative leaders in higher education who seek guidance in dealing with today's complexity, opportunities, and demands. It is also addressed to those who aspire to hold positions of leadership and to the many faculty and staff members who serve in informal leadership roles within their departments, disciplines, or institutions. Additionally, the book serves as a guide and resource for those responsible for the design and implementation of leadership development programs in higher education.

22883 Quicksilver Drive
Sterling, VA 20166-2019   Subscribe to our e-mail alerts: www.Styluspub.com

Also available from Stylus

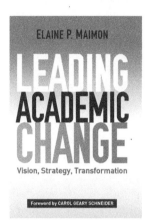

Leading Academic Change

Vision, Strategy, Transformation

Elaine P. Maimon

Foreword by Carol Geary Schneider

"One of America's best university presidents has written a brilliant book that will surely inspire and instruct other educational leaders. Each page overflows with eloquence, wisdom, evidence, and powerful examples. This book is perhaps Maimon's most significant gift to higher education. Anyone interested in transformation must read it." —*Shaun R. Harper, Clifford and Betty Allen Professor, University of Southern California Rossier School of Education*

Written by a sitting college president who has presided over transformative change at a state university, this book takes on the big questions and issues of change and change management, what needs to be done and how to do it. Writing in a highly accessible style, the author recommends changes for higher education such as the reallocation of resources to support full-time faculty members in foundation-level courses, navigable pathways from community college to the university, infusion rather than proliferation of courses, and the role of state universities in countering the disappearance of the middle class. The book describes how these changes can be made, as well as why we must make them if our society is to thrive in the twenty-first century.

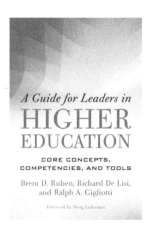

A Guide for Leaders in Higher Education

Core Concepts, Competencies, and Tools

Brent D. Ruben, Richard De Lisi, and Ralph A. Gigliotti

Foreword by Doug Lederman

At a time when higher education faces the unprecedented challenges of declining revenues and increased scrutiny; questions about access, cost, and the value of degrees; and the imperative to educate a more diverse student body, there is

(Continues on preceding page)

INSIDE
HIGHER ED

Inside Higher Ed is the leading source for the latest news, thought leadership, careers, and resources for the entire higher education community. Since our founding in 2004, we have not wavered from our mission. We serve all of higher education—individuals, institutions, corporations, and nonprofits—so they can do their jobs better, transforming their lives and those of the students they serve. We remain a fiercely independent voice, providing thoughtful, substantive analysis on the pressing issues facing higher education.

Inside Higher Ed was founded in 2004 by three executives with decades of expertise in higher education journalism and recruitment. We conceived of *Inside Higher Ed* with a few underlying principles:

Excellence. We believe deeply in the many missions of colleges and universities: shaping minds, training workers, engaging in discovery. To carry out those missions, the people who work in higher education need the best news and information possible about their professional world. By *best*, we mean above all accurate, thorough, and reliable. We care about history, about context, about nuance—but we also take our watchdog role seriously and will do plenty of hard-hitting investigative reporting, sparing no sacred cows.

Accessibility. Our content is freely accessible—so everyone can be an insider. Jobseekers, too, can use virtually all of our services without paying a dime. And employers will find a comprehensive suite of jobs services at prices that every institution can afford.

Community. If we're doing our jobs well, everyone who works in or cares about higher education should feel, every day, that this site is produced for them. This is a gathering place for all of the many constituents and diverse institutions that make up the rich web of higher education. We invite you—no, actively encourage you— to add your views to our mix.

Drop us a line at info@insidehighered.com.